The Dominican Republic

The Dominican Republic

BY LURA ROGERS AND
BARBARA RADCLIFFE ROGERS

Enchantment of the World
Second Series

Children's Press®

A Division of Grolier Publishing

NEW YORK   LONDON   HONG KONG   SYDNEY
DANBURY, CONNECTICUT

Frontispiece: Carnival

Consultant: Ernesto Sagás, Ph.D., adjunct assistant professor, The City University of
                New York and Rutgers University

Please note: *All statistics are as up-to-date as possible at the time of publication.*

Visit Children's Press on the Internet: http://publishing.grolier.com

Book design by Ox+Company, Inc.

Library of Congress Cataloging-in-Publication Data

Rogers, Lura.
    The Dominican Republic / by Lura Rogers and Barbara Radcliffe
    Rogers.
      p.   cm. — (Enchantment of the world. Second series)
    Includes bibliographical references and index.
    Summary: Describes the geography, history, culture, religion, and
  people of the Caribbean island nation of the Dominican Republic.
    ISBN 0-516-21125-0
    1. Dominican Republic—Juvenile literature. [1. Dominican
    Republic.]
  I. Rogers, Barbara Radcliffe. II. Title. III. Series.
  F1934.2.R64 1999
  972.93—dc21   98-37087
                                                          CIP
                                                           AC

Acknowledgments

The authors would like to thank the staff at the Keene Public Library, in Keene, New Hampshire, especially Dottie Howard, Nancy Baldvins, Charlotte Lesser, and Nancy Vincent, and Teri Weston at the Crandall Public Library in Glens Falls, New York, for their help in ferreting out hard-to-find facts and statistics. They would also like to thank their friend and colleague, Sylvia McNair, and their editor, Halley Gatenby.

This book is dedicated to Eric, with whom I hope to share the world some day. —Lura

Contents

Cover photo:
Terra cotta dolls from
the cities of Moca and
La Vega

Colonial Santo Domingo

An angelfish

Island in the Winds

Farmlands of Cordillera Septentrional, the Dominican Republic's northern mountains

THE DOMINICAN REPUBLIC, on the island of Hispaniola, is the gateway to the Caribbean in more ways than one. It is not only at the geographical entrance to this watery playground, but learning about Hispaniola helps us understand its island neighbors, too. The modern history of the New World began here.

Its tree-clad mountains, its valleys, and its long, beautiful beaches look much like those of the other islands. Its lively mix of people, with their merengue music and upbeat attitude, represent the island cultures well. When you know the Dominicans, you are well on your way to knowing the Caribbean.

The trade winds, those air currents that filled the sails of ships carrying explorers from the Old World to the New, could just as well be called the winds of change. The ships that rode those winds straight toward the Dominican shore carried people, plants, animals, and ideas that would change Hispaniola and the other islands of the West Indies forever.

Opposite: **Playa Grande on the Amber Coast**

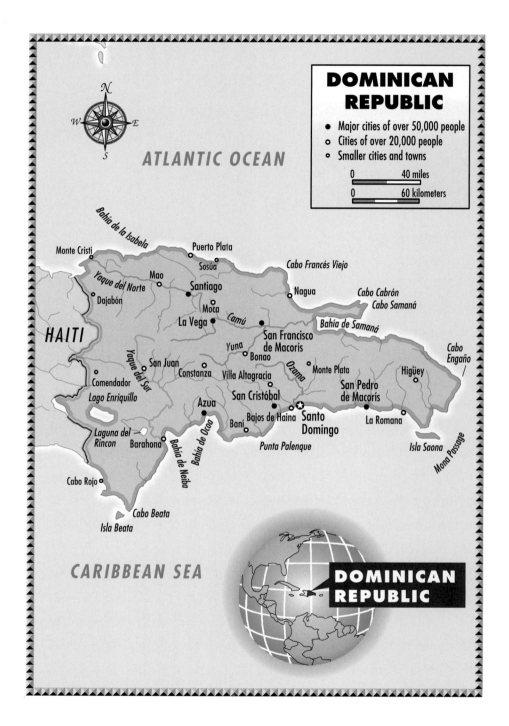

Geopolitical map of
the Dominican Republic

Five hundred years ago, the trade winds blew three tiny ships from Spain—the *Niña*, the *Pinta*, and the *Santa María*—to establish the first permanent European colony in the New World. From that time, it seemed as though everyone who drifted westward from Europe stopped here to trade or raid.

Hispaniola's position in the world's sea lanes would affect its fortunes again, centuries later, when the United States feared the revolution brewing there would be a threat to the new Panama Canal. Once again, the Dominican Republic was directly in the path of ships. This time, the ships were headed from both European and North American ports to the passage between the Atlantic and the Pacific.

As you will see, not all the changes blown in by these winds have been bad. Absorbing the best from the peoples that have settled there, the Dominican Republic has taken its place among the nations of the world. It has grown and changed. To these winds it owes the lively rhythms of its culture and its charming Old World Spanish ways. Today, travelers still come here from all over the world, but no longer to trade and raid. Instead, these new travelers stay and play.

Island in the Winds **11**

Mountaintops
in the Sea

THE DOMINICAN REPUBLIC OCCUPIES the eastern two-thirds of the island of Hispaniola. This island, like all the islands in the West Indies, was formed by the peaks of the Greater Antilles mountain chain, whose bases are deep beneath the sea. Hispaniola is about 575 miles (925 kilometers) southeast of Miami, Florida. The Atlantic Ocean forms its northern coast, while the warm waters of the Caribbean Sea wash the southern shore. To the east lies the treacherous Mona Passage, a rough stretch of water that separates Hispaniola from the island of Puerto Rico. The country of Haiti lies to the west, taking up one-third of the island.

The Dominican Republic covers an area of 18,816 square miles (48,734 sq km), which is almost as big as New Hampshire and Vermont combined, or a little smaller than Nova Scotia. Miles of white sandy beaches line its coasts, and chains of beautiful mountains rise farther inland.

The shores of Cayo Levantado in Samaná Bay

Opposite: **The countryside in the Cordillera Central**

Geographical Features

Area: 18,816 square miles (48,734 sq km)

Coastline: 800 miles (1,288 km)

Highest Elevation: *Pico Duarte* (Duarte Peak), 10,417 feet (3,175 m)

Lowest Elevation: *Lago Enriquillo* (Lake Enriquillo), 150 feet (46 m) below sea level

Largest Lake: *Lago Enriquillo* (Lake Enriquillo), 25 miles (40 km) long

Longest River: *Yaque del Norte*, 184 miles (296 km) long

Average Temperature: in July, 81°F (27°C); in January, 75°F (24°C)

Average Annual Rainfall: in mountains, 100 inches (254 cm); in valleys, 50 inches (127 cm)

Greatest Distance from East to West: 240 miles (386 km)

Greatest Distance from North to South: 170 miles (274 km)

Largest City: Santo Domingo

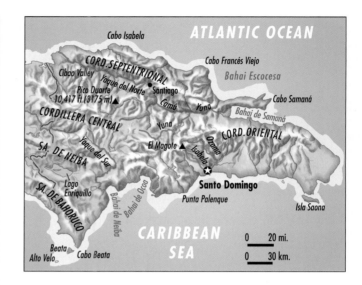

Rivers flowing down the mountains create fertile valleys that are ideal for farming. Although tourism and abuse of the land's resources have changed many regions, much of the island remains almost unchanged since the first Europeans saw it 500 years ago.

A Peak at the Mountains

Four major mountain chains spread across the western half of the island. The largest of these is the Cordillera Central, which rises proudly to the highest point in the West Indies, *Pico Duarte* (Duarte Peak). At 10,417 feet (3,175 m), it is sometimes covered with a layer of frost that makes it appear snow-covered. This mountain range is the backbone of the central region. To the north, the Cordillera Septentrional rises from the plains along the Atlantic coast. In contrast to

the grand peaks of the central range, its highest mountains reach 3,300 feet (1,006 m). In the southwest, the Sierra de Neiba and the Sierra de Bahoruco overlook a lake-filled valley.

Valle del Río Bao, in the Cordillera Central

Juan Pablo Duarte

Pico Duarte, the highest point in the West Indies, was named for Juan Pablo Duarte, a leader of the independence movement that freed the Dominican Republic from the rule of Haiti. Duarte was born into a wealthy family and spent seven years studying overseas. When he returned in 1833, this idealist determined to free his people from tyranny. In 1838, Duarte and a group of like-minded Dominicans formed a secret society called *La Trinitaria*. They were opposed to the harsh rule of Haitian dictator Jean-Pierre Boyer and spent years plotting to overthrow him. Finally, Duarte's followers captured the capital city of Santo Domingo and declared independence for the Dominican Republic on February 27, 1844. The statue at left honors Duarte.

Water from the Mountains

The Yaque del Norte River in the Central Mountains is an important source of water for the city of Santiago.

Most of the Dominican Republic's major rivers spring from the mountains of the Cordillera Central. The Yaque del Norte begins at an elevation of 8,462 feet (2,579 m), near Pico Duarte, running 184 miles (296 km) until reaching the sea at

Montecristi on the northwest coast. This river is the major source of soil nutrients and irrigation water for the valley below. It also supplies water for the city of Santiago.

The Yaque del Sur falls from the southern side of Pico Duarte, beginning at an elevation of over 8,500 feet (2,591 m). For about three-quarters of its length it flows through the mountains, finally reaching Neiba Bay on the southern coast. The Isabela and Ozama Rivers begin in the lower regions east of the Cordillera Central, meeting the sea at Santo Domingo.

A dark tobacco field ready for harvest in the Río Yaque Valley, Cibao region

Beneath the Slopes

The Cibao Valley lies below the southern slopes of the Cordillera Septentrional. This fertile region covers 150 square miles (388 sq km). The Yaque del Norte Basin provides nutrients for the land by depositing soil washed down from the mountains during heavy rainfalls. Its water irrigates the valley's cropland. The city of Santiago overlooks the Vega Real, at the eastern end of the Cibao Valley. The rich soil of this region makes it a major center for growing tobacco and grains.

The Neiba Valley is in the southwest, surrounded by two mountain chains that were once separated by a strait—a narrow passage of water. As land shifted, a pocket of saltwater was trapped to form what is now known as *Lago Enriquillo* (Lake Enriquillo), the largest lake on the island. Larger than Manhattan Island, Lago Enriquillo stretches for 25 miles (40 km) and is home to crocodiles and other wildlife. At 150 feet (46 m) below sea level, it is the lowest point in the West Indies. The protected land surrounding the lake, called the *Hoya de Enriquillo* region, is known for its hot, dry climate.

The Amber Coast

The northern coast of the Dominican Republic is named for the fossilized resin called amber. The world's richest supply of amber is found in the hills along the coast, where it has been forming for millions of years. Amber is created when resins from pine trees oxidize, or combine with oxygen, and are buried underground or underwater. Over time, the resin fossilizes and becomes a hard, yellow-brown substance. Insects that were trapped in the sticky resin millions of years ago are sometimes found inside the amber, perfectly preserved. Amber is often polished to make jewelry.

The opening scene from the movie *Jurassic Park*, in which DNA is extracted from an amber-trapped insect, was filmed on the Amber Coast of the Dominican Republic. The amber featured in the movie is the oldest-known piece in the world.

Santo Domingo

On the southern coast, where the Ozama and Isabela Rivers meet the sea, sits the capital city of Santo Domingo. This site was chosen for its protected harbor and convenient location close to the gold mines, overlooking the Caribbean Sea. With a population of 2,411,895, the city struggles to keep up with the increasing number of people who move there. Many come to the city in hopes of finding work, but instead they find

housing shortages and a poor water supply. Santo Domingo is also home to a growing middle class, a relatively new group in the Dominican Republic.

The obelisk in Santo Domingo faces the Caribbean Sea.

The Cathedral and Duarte Park in Santiago

Santiago

Santiago lies in the center of the Cibao Valley region on the Yaque del Norte river in the northwest part of the country. Today, it is the Dominican Republic's agricultural center, and located in the heart of the country's tobacco-growing region. Local landmarks include the Monument to the Restoration Heroes, the Cathedral of Santiago, Pontifical Catholic University *Madre y Maestra*, and a tobacco museum.

Looking at Dominican Cities

Santiago de los Caballeros (known simply as Santiago) was founded in 1494, destroyed by an earthquake in 1564, and then rebuilt. Landmarks include the Monument to the Restoration Heroes and the Cathedral of Santiago. It has a population of 490,000. Its average January temperature is 75°F (24°C), and its average July temperature is 80°F (26°C).

Puerto Plata was founded on the north coast in 1502. Its population of 85,400 enjoys average temperatures of 73°F (23°C) in January and 78°F (25°C) in July. San Felipe, a colonial fort, is a well-known landmark.

La Romana, east of Santo Domingo on the south coast, has a population of 101,350. Average temperatures range from 75°F (24°C) in January to 81°F (27°C) in July. Landmarks include Altos de Chavón, a modern village built of stone in a variety of historic styles. It includes a design school, and a well-known tourist resort called Casa del Campo.

Coastal Cities

The coastal town of Puerto Plata is popular for its beautiful beaches and very important to the Dominican tourism industry. It sits near Mount Isabel de Torres, whose peak reaches

Central Park in Puerto Plata. San Felipe Church is visible in the background.

Boats on a river of the southeast coast in La Romana

The buildings at Altos de
Chavón were constructed to
appear old-fashioned.

2,600 feet (792 m). A cable car carries visitors to the top for a view over the city and the Atlantic Ocean. The city was originally founded nearby as Isabela in 1493, but in 1496 the Europeans moved their headquarters to what is now the capital, Santo Domingo. Because of the heavy flow of tourists in the past 25 years, Puerto Plata and the surrounding beaches have become overdeveloped, crowded with foreign-owned resort hotels.

The history of La Romana, a seaport east of Santo Domingo on the south coast, is closely intertwined with the multinational company Gulf and Western. Until the 1980s, Gulf and Western just about owned the town, from which it managed its sugar-growing and refining, cattle-raising, and cement businesses. Following criticism of its operations there, the company spent millions of dollars to improve the town's schools, hospitals, and housing.

Hurricanes—Tropical Killers

Once every two years, on average, a serious hurricane hits the island of Hispaniola. Houses are upturned, roofs blown off, windows shattered. Wind, heavy surf, and flooding uproot trees and destroy croplands.

All hurricanes begin as tropical storms, though not all storms become hurricanes. A hurricane begins when the temperature of the top layer of seawater rises above 80°F (27°C). The water begins to evaporate and clouds form.

Winds then pick up the clouds, spinning them in a circular motion, and an eye, or whirlwind, begins to develop. In a mature hurricane, the eye is a cylinder of low-pressure air surrounded by clouds. The eye can be up to 20 miles (32 km) in diameter.

Once the winds reach 74 miles (119 k) per hour, the storm is officially a hurricane. The air pressure inside and under the storm is constantly changing. Hurricanes last from

three to fourteen days and move at 5 to 20 miles (8 to 32 k) per hour. They die out over land, where the ocean water cannot continue to feed them. Most of the hurricanes that hit the Caribbean develop in the Atlantic Ocean between South America and Africa. Each storm is named according to an alphabetical list made at the beginning of the season.

In September 1998, Hurricane Georges battered the island of Hispaniola with wind and torrents of rain that washed away entire mountainsides. When the storm finally ended, 500 people in the Dominican Republic were dead or missing, 500 others were seriously injured, 287,000 people were left homeless, and 80 percent of the country's crops and livestock had been washed away. Early estimates suggested damages reaching $6 billion— all from one storm.

A Town Built by Refugees

The town of Sosúa was established in 1939 by a small group of Jewish refugees, most of them from Austria. During World War II (1939–1945), Dominican president Rafael Trujillo invited European Jews escaping persecution under Hitler to come to the Dominican Republic, promising them land on the northern coast. They had to clear the land to farm on it, but a number settled there and began dairy farms. To this day, some of their descendants live in Sosúa, and there is a small synagogue on the town's main street, as well as a museum dedicated to its history.

In 1991, original settlers and their relatives returned from all over the world to celebrate the anniversary of the founding of Sosúa. Although an overwhelming percentage of the island's population is Roman Catholic, this Jewish community never met with discrimination. Sosúa's milk and cheese are appreciated for being safe to eat, which is not always true of dairy foods in the Caribbean.

When It Rains, It Pours

The Dominican Republic has a hot, tropical climate with fresh winds. Average temperatures range from 75°F (24°C) in January to 81°F (27°C) in July. Along the coast and in protected valleys, temperatures can reach 100°F (37°C), and the mountains can get as cold as 32°F (0°C). Trade winds off the sea help to cool the coast.

The weather is divided into rainy and dry seasons. During the rainy season, which lasts from May to November, storms come and go quickly, drenching the land and cooling the air. The mountain regions get up to 100 inches (254 cm) of rain in a year, while the Neiba Valley sees only half that much. The average rainfall for the plains is 60 inches (152 cm).

Tropical storms and depressions are common, but the biggest threat is hurricanes. At their worst in August and September, these huge storms create winds of up to 125 miles (201 km) per hour, destroying crops and homes. The southwestern part of the island is hit the hardest. In 1930, a devastating hurricane brought winds of 200 miles (322 km) per hour. It caused $15 million in damage to the city of Santo Domingo alone. Hurricane David hit Santo Domingo in 1979 killing 2,000 people on its three-day rampage. In 1998, Hurricane Georges devastated parts of the country.

Natural Neighbors

26

A WIDE VARIETY OF PLANT AND ANIMAL LIFE IS FOUND within the borders of the small country of the Dominican Republic, thanks to its dramatically different areas of climate. Habitats range from beaches and mountaintops to deserts and rain forests. Each of these zones holds its own kinds of trees, plants, birds, and animals.

The coastal waters add thousands of species to the list of wildlife that share the island with humans. Many living things that thrive here are native to the island, but some were imported by Europeans, mostly food crops and trees. This combination makes the island's flora and fauna an interesting mix.

Greenery and Gardens

The first thing visitors notice is the amazing variety of plants. More than 5,600 species are found here. The plant life changes with the elevation and the climate. The cooler, mountainous regions are home to big, strong trees, while the plants and trees of the rain forests need plenty of moisture and shade to survive. In the drier deserts, plants must store water, as cactus plants do, in order to survive the long dry season. The rich land of the Cibao Valley is a prime growing area, covered in crops.

The cashew plant is native to this country.

Opposite: **A brightly colored queen angelfish surrounded by coral**

Reaching altitudes over 10,000 feet (3,048 m), the mountains often resemble those of the northeastern United States, with their covering of coniferous, or cone-bearing trees such as the native Creolan pine. Pine forests cover approximately 2,500 square miles (6,475 sq km), twice as much land as the state of Rhode Island. The *Reserva Científica Valle Nuevo* (New Valley Scientific Reserve) protects stands of virgin forest—where the trees have never been cut down.

When star fruit is cut in half, the interior resembles the shape of a star.

The climate on the lower mountainsides is warmer, and covered with lush rain forests. Exotic trees including mahogany, satinwood, and ebony grow here, although some areas have been almost completely stripped of these precious woods. Rain forests are also home to cedar, juniper, and lignum vitae. These areas provide a perfect habitat for native food-bearing plants, such as star apple, wild guava, wild pepper, calabash, cashew, and soursop. Mahogany from the eastern mountains was used to build the first cathedral in the New World. Mangrove trees grow in the swamps.

Along the beaches, native royal palms spread their leaves over the hot sand, shading beachgoers. The coconut palm also grows along the water, where it was planted after being imported from Africa. In the dry deserts, plant life is mostly limited to cactus and the agave plant. In areas with a moderate climate, the Dominican magnolia grows, along with the ceiba, or silk-cotton tree, which can live for 300 years.

Before the Europeans arrived, the Taíno people cultivated the indigenous crops—plants native to the island—and developed fairly advanced farming skills. They used the *higüero* (cal-abash) tree for food and dried its gourds to make masks and containers. The *yuca* (cassava) plant was their main food, and they also grew papaya,

The water from these coconuts is a popular drink for both Dominicans and tourists.

Calabash gourds have hard shells which are used as utensils.

Farms versus Forests

Despite its wide variety of plant life, deforestation is a serious problem in the Dominican Republic. Slash-and-burn farming, officially prohibited since the 1970s, seriously damages the forests and land.

In slash-and-burn farming, every few years, families abandon their small plots of land and burn down tree-covered mountain slopes to make new garden plots. Although the soil is relatively good at first, full of natural fertilizer from decaying tree leaves, it soon becomes as poor as the old. Without tree roots to hold the topsoil on the sloping fields, rainwater washes it away.

In 1973, the United Nations estimated that only 16 percent of the Dominican Republic was forested. Today, although reforestation has helped to put back some trees, only 13 percent of the land is wooded. The lumber industry and hurricanes are now the major enemies of the forests.

pepper, and tobacco. It was here that the Europeans were first introduced to tobacco.

Most of the plants introduced from outside the island have adapted without disrupting the ecological balance. Surprisingly, the country's biggest cash crop, sugarcane, was imported by the Europeans, along with cocoa, coffee, bananas, and mangoes. Many crops came from other parts of the world that were being explored at the time. As a result, crops grown in the Dominican Republic include the Australian eucalyptus, almonds from India, and breadfruit from the Pacific Islands. Nearby Central and South America, which were being settled by the Spanish at the same time as the Dominican Republic, were the source of citrus fruits and cocoa. Only about 35 percent of the 5,600 plant species found on the island today were there when explorers first landed.

Fins, Feathers, and Fur

The wildlife of the Dominican Republic includes not only land creatures and fantastic birds, but also vast ecosystems of freshwater and saltwater life. Most are native to the island, although the Europeans did bring in some animals. These imported animals did far more damage to the ecological balance than the imported plants did.

Lago Enriquillo is one of the most interesting habitats because it is a saltwater lake. American crocodiles live here, as well as rhinoceros iguanas and variegated-shell turtles. The fish population has declined recently as the water has become gradually saltier. It is now three times as salty as the ocean.

An American crocodile

Alligators and crocodiles also live in other Dominican waters.

The warm waters off the Caribbean and Atlantic coasts have some of the world's most interesting ocean life. Crabs and snails live along the beaches and tidal pools, while the oceans are filled with fish—some smaller than your little finger and others that weigh more than 100 volumes of the *Encyclopedia Britannica*. The water is filled with shrimp, mullet, red snapper, sardines, mackerel, and oysters, all of which find their way onto Dominican dinner plates. Turtles, barracuda, eels, parrotfish, and sawfish also cruise the waters.

The extensive coral reefs along the coast are created by tiny animals called *anthozoans*. These creatures produce calcium carbonate, forming the large, delicate coral reefs. Coral reefs need a perfect ecological balance to survive, and in spite of damage done by soil runoff from deforested mountains, the reefs along the shore of the Dominican Republic are in good condition. Not only are they a beautiful spot for divers and swimmers, but reefs form a protective barrier between shallow-water creatures and the more dangerous deep-sea wildlife.

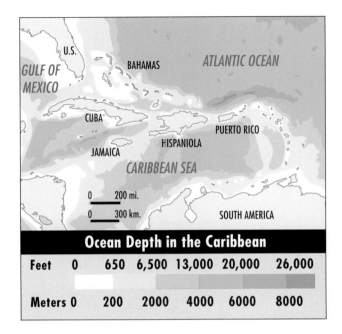

Ocean Depth in the Caribbean					
Feet 0	650	6,500	13,000	20,000	26,000
Meters 0	200	2000	4000	6000	8000

A banded butterfly fish surrounded by colorful coral

From December through March, humpback whales visit the Dominican coast just off *Bahía de Samaná* (Samaná Bay). Bottle-nosed dolphins can also be seen swimming playfully, a favorite attraction for both visitors and Dominicans. The endangered Caribbean manatees move slowly through the coastal waters, feeding on plant life. Although fishing

A Cow That Swims?

Affectionately called the "sea cow," the manatee is a peaceful inhabitant of the coastal waters. This mild-tempered mammal eats up to 100 pounds (45 kg) of water plants a day, using its upper lip, which is divided in half like a pair of pliers. The manatee has gray skin and bristly hairs, with front legs shaped like paddles. Its tail is rounded and it has no hind legs. The Caribbean species grows up to 13 feet (4 m) long and weighs about 3,500 pounds (1,600 kg). As a result of hunting, the gentle manatee is now an endangered species.

A flock of pink flamingoes

has depleted much of the ocean wildlife, many areas away from the populated coastal towns are still literally swimming with life.

Along the coast and the shore of Lago Enriquillo, pink flamingos brighten the blue waters and the beaches. The 2,000 species of birds in the Dominican Republic include everything from herons to the rare Hispaniolan parrot. Ducks and pelicans live near the water, and in the forest many types of brilliant parrots fly from tree to tree. Exotic nightingales sing alongside more commonplace swallows and pigeons. The island also has a population of ibis and spoonbills.

Los Haitises National Park, on Samaná Bay, is a bird sanctuary and historical site. Many beautiful rare birds can be found here among the extensive caves that hold inscriptions

Los Haitises National Park on Samaná Bay

The rhinoceros iguana is an endangered species.

left by the Taíno people. One "bird" that populates the island thickly is unwelcome, though—the mosquito. It is not only a nuisance but may also carry malaria, a serious disease.

The Spanish brought cows and pigs as livestock and donkeys and horses for work. Rats and mice were uninvited stowaways on ships, so the Spanish brought cats and mongooses to help control them. The European animals upset the balance of the island's ecology so much that many species have been lost entirely or are endangered.

Friend or Foe?

The mongoose is a small mammal that usually grows to a length of about 16 inches (41 cm). Its stiff yellow-tan hair has brown and black hairs mixed in. This feisty little animal is not a native of Hispaniola. Early European settlers of this and many other islands, including Jamaica, Puerto Rico, and Hawaii, imported the mongoose to control rodents. The mongoose is quick, fierce-tempered, and agile and can kill rats and snakes easily. It also eats birds, eggs, and small animals. What settlers did not realize, however, was how quickly the mongooses would multiply and disturb the natural balance. They have destroyed a large percentage of the native bird population and are now considered a pest themselves.

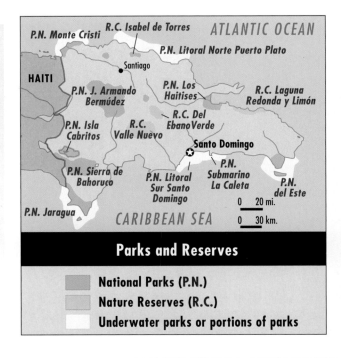

Among the indigenous species that remain are many kinds of reptiles, rodents, and insects. The rhinoceros iguana and the ricard iguana, both endangered species, inhabit the warmer zones. Snakes, lizards, and noisy little frogs can be found all over. The solendon, a small, scaled rodent that resembles an anteater, eats insects. It is nearly extinct now, along with its rodent relative—the jutía. The agouti, a pesky rodent that eats sugarcane, is one of the few rodents the mongoose does not hunt.

Making Pigs of Themselves on Local Plants

No one knows exactly what became of the 8 pigs that Columbus unloaded from his ship and left on the island of Hispaniola in 1493. But historians do know that 24 pigs brought to the neighboring island of Cuba in 1498 had multiplied to 30,000 by the year 1514. The two islands have similar climates and the same plants for pigs to root up and eat, so it is reasonable to guess that by 1509 the Spanish colonists on the island could have been well fed with 10,000 pigs.

A Journey through Time

Opposite: **The sixteenth-century fortress of San Felipe at Puerto Plata**

Long before the Spanish explorer Christopher Columbus (Cristóbal Colón in Spanish) set foot on the island of Hispaniola, this beautiful land was home to a large number of peaceful people. The European influences on the island quickly changed their way of life.

The culture underwent periods of chaos and unrest as the people struggled between foreign rule and self-government. After periods of U.S. occupation and a dictatorship, this small country finally began to get on its feet as a democracy, for the first time successful at keeping peace within its borders.

A wooden Taíno idol, or *zemí*, found in Santo Domingo

Discovery

Hispaniola was discovered by a group of people from South America between 3000 and 4000 B.C. Nearly 3,000 years later, people from the Arawak tribe of the Orinoco Valley (in what is now Venezuela) came to the island. They settled on its eastern tip, which they called *Quisqueya*. More Arawaks arrived over the next centuries, gradually mixing with the original settlers. These people, who settled on the island and developed an agricultural society, called themselves the *Taíno*, which means "good" or "noble." They used this name to distinguish themselves from the more warlike Arawaks, called

A Taíno petroglyph, or carving, inscribed on coral rocks. The petroglyphs were the Taíno's sole means of written communication.

the Caribs, who arrived later. The Caribs were fighters who roamed the Caribbean.

The Taíno used farming techniques to improve their crops. They cultivated corn, sweet potatoes, beans, squash, and cassava for food, heaping mounds of soil into rows as beds for the crops. As well as food, the Taíno cultivated cotton, tobacco, and calabash—a large gourd used to make containers for food and water. From the ceiba tree, they constructed long canoes that held up to 150 people. They had simple wooden houses with thatched roofs, called *bohíos*.

Their society was organized into small villages housing 1,000 to 2,000 people, with a village chief called a *cacique*. The chief could be either male or female. The villages were grouped into regional chiefdoms, each with its own leader. Unlike the system used in the United States and Canada, the lineage of a family was traced back through the mother's side, not the father's. The Taíno had no written language, so we know very little about how they lived.

By the time Europeans landed on the island, there were at least 500,000 inhabitants (some believe it was closer to 1 million) living in a peaceful and well-organized culture.

Taíno Beliefs

The head of the Taíno religion was Atabey, the goddess of freshwater and fertility. She was the mother of Yucahú, the lord of the cassava tree and the sea. Lesser deities called *zemís* lived all around them. The Taíno carried fetishes of these lesser gods for their protection and blessings. Fetishes are small objects believed to have special powers. The Taíno believed that ancestral spirits lived with them in the natural world.

A Cloud from the East

In 1493, the Spanish explorer Christopher Columbus landed on the northern coast of the island, which he had visited on his first exploration in 1492. The town of Isabela was founded where he landed and became Spain's Caribbean base for a short time. In 1496, the capital was moved to the southern coast by Christopher's brother Bartholomew. Santo Domingo became an important Spanish base for trade and exploration, as well as the political center of the Spanish empire.

Columbus and the Spanish colonists liked this island for its convenient location, its gold, and its mild-mannered natives, who were easy to control as a labor force. Columbus was appointed governor by the king and queen of Spain, and Spanish adventurers began to arrive to mine the gold. As governor, Columbus tried to limit the abuse of the local natives by these new settlers. But the settlers complained and the Spanish king established a new system that allowed almost unlimited

A painting by Cabral-Bejarano of Christopher Columbus with his ships, the *Niña*, the *Pinta*, and the *Santa María*.

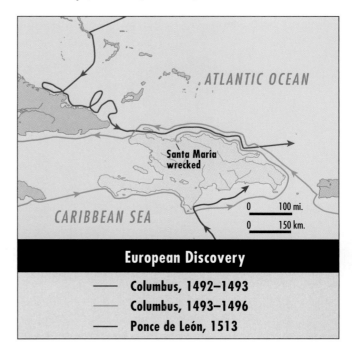

ATLANTIC OCEAN

Santa María wrecked

CARIBBEAN SEA

0   100 mi.
0   150 km.

European Discovery

—— Columbus, 1492–1493
—— Columbus, 1493–1496
—— Ponce de León, 1513

The statue of Christopher Columbus in Columbus Square, Santo Domingo

La Isabela, the site where the Spaniards founded the first city in America. Native Indians are buried here.

exploitation of the local people. This system, called *encomienda*, distributed the lands—and the natives—among the settlers, who used the natives as slaves.

The Spanish conquerors couldn't get along with one another though, and by 1500, Hispaniola was in civil war. When Spanish military leader Francisco Bobadilla arrived, he found such civil chaos that he arrested the Columbus brothers and sent them back to Spain to answer to the queen. He restored order with a heavy hand, and under his harsh rule, royal mines were established using slave labor. The gold his mines produced did him little good. A ship carrying Bobadilla and 600 pounds (272 kg) of gold was wrecked on its way back to Spain in 1502, and both he and the gold were lost.

From 1502 until 1509, Nicolás de Ovando ruled, spreading tyranny throughout the island. He treated the natives brutally, and began bringing slaves from Africa in 1503 to replace them when they died. As well as oppression, the Europeans brought new diseases. The Taíno had no natural defenses against these diseases and most of them died. Others committed suicide to escape their hopeless situation. Although a small Taíno rebellion erupted in 1495, it was quickly stamped out, and by 1524, only thirty years after Columbus established the colony, the Taíno people were nearly wiped out.

A Third Columbus Arrives

After de Ovando, Spain sent Christopher Columbus's son, Diego, to govern the colony. Although Diego Columbus spent much of his time in Spain, the Crown became nervous that he would abuse his power and established an *audiencia* (council) on the island in 1512. This council acted as a watchdog over the governor, with power to review and control his policies.

A night view of the colonial area of Santo Domingo reflected on the Ozama River

The council took over many of Diego's powers, and stayed in place long after the end of his rule in 1526.

But Diego Columbus was an active leader and ordered the construction of the Alcázar, the first European fortress in the Americas. Later, in 1538, the first university in the New World was built. By this time, the labor force was entirely African, and slaves built the rising city of Santo Domingo. Despite their earlier efforts in Hispaniola, Spain had nearly deserted the entire western end of the island by the end of the 1500s. The land fell into the hands of local landowners who ruled their property with little control from the island government.

As Spain's attention turned to its colonies on the mainland of South and Central America, pirates and ambitious explorers saw the opportunity to exploit the island. In 1586, the British explorer Sir Francis Drake seized Santo Domingo and demanded a ransom from the Spanish government for its return. Many pirates, including the infamous Blackbeard, made the island their stamping grounds, and it became headquarters for some. Because of the many harbors where ships could hide, and the government's poor organization, illegal trade was often carried on and smugglers made a good living here.

An Island Adrift

Spain was losing its grip on Hispaniola. French troops occupied the eastern end of the island, and fought with the Spanish for control of the rest. Although the Treaty of Ryswick ended Spain's war with France in 1697, and returned the two armies to opposite ends of Hispaniola, Spain did not give up its claim on the French-held land. Not until 80 years later, by the Treaty of Aranjuez, did Spain finally recognize the French claim and agree to a formal border between the two colonies.

A depiction of a restrained African slave being prepared for transport

Between 1761 and 1810, more than 6,000 slaves were brought from Africa. During this time, a revolution to end slavery was brewing in Saint-Dominique, as the French end of the island was known. In 1801, black slaves led by Toussaint-Louverture rebelled against the French and soon took over the entire island. Toussaint-Louverture had fought in the name of freedom for slaves, but faced with a country impoverished from years of war and neglect, he soon began to rule as a dictator. He set up a labor system that was close to slavery. When a new constitution gave him full power, he established plantation systems that were just as brutal as the previous plantations had been. Internal passports prevented black workers from moving from one town to another.

A 1913 portrait of Toussaint-Louverture by Giradin

Meanwhile, Napoleon Bonaparte, fresh from victories in Europe, wanted land in North America. To do so, he needed a strong base in the Caribbean to control sea access to southern ports. Hispaniola commanded the gateway to the Caribbean, and Napoleon sent an army to reclaim the island from the black revolutionaries. He expected little resistance

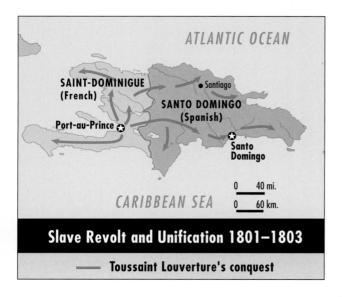

Slave Revolt and Unification 1801–1803

— Toussaint Louverture's conquest

from the former French colony, but he was mistaken. Toussaint-Louverture's army fought fiercely, but they finally surrendered.

France now officially occupied the entire island, but the French troops were weakened by yellow fever, and the two parts of the island began to separate again. In 1822, Jean-Pierre Boyer became president and Haitians again occupied the whole island. Boyer ruled for twenty-one years, neglecting the country so badly that the few remaining plantations were ruined and schools and universities closed.

Independence at Last

In 1838, a small group of Dominican intellectuals organized *La Trinitaria*, a secret society designed to overthrow Haitian rule and gain independence. The society was established by Juan Pablo Duarte, the son of a wealthy Dominican family. Its three leaders were Duarte, Francisco del Rosario Sánchez, and Ramón Matías Mella. On February 27, 1844, revolutionaries led by Mella seized Santo Domingo. Independence was declared and the Dominican Republic was born.

Pedro Santana, one of the leaders in the revolution, became the first president. After seeing a constitution adopted, he

Independence was declared at El Conde Gate in Santo Domingo.

resigned in 1848 to become head of the military. He wanted to prevent another Haitian takeover. Buenaventura Báez was his successor, but the two competed for control. By 1861, the presidency had changed hands between them so often that the nation was torn apart by political unrest. Santana asked Queen Isabela II of Spain for help. He thought that, as a Spanish colony, the Dominican Republic would be in a stronger position opposing Haiti.

Spanish troops arrived, but this "help" didn't work as well as Santana had hoped. Spain imposed new taxes and ruled harshly. However, yellow fever swept through the Spanish troops, and armies of rebels rose up everywhere. In 1865, the Spanish eventually lost the War for the Restoration of the Republic to the rebels and withdrew. The four-year period when the Dominican Republic again became a Spanish colony is known as *La Anexión a España*.

Over the next seventeen years, the presidency changed hands twelve times, and various regions of the Dominican Republic fought among themselves. In 1882, Ulises Heureaux was named president.

Heureaux ruled as a tyrant, although he managed to improve communications by building some railways and installing cables and a telegraph system. However, these projects, and his own personal greed, were financed by international loans, and the nation was soon in serious debt. In 1899, Heureaux was assassinated. Most of the next two decades were years of total anarchy—a constant battle between the two major political groups of the time.

Connecting islets in Samaná Bay

A Plea for Help

As world attention was drawn toward the Panama Canal, U.S. President Theodore Roosevelt recognized that unrest in the Dominican Republic, with its prominent position on shipping routes, was a threat to the project. He used the country's crippling foreign debt as a way to influence the unstable nation and suggested U.S. financial intervention. In 1905, President Carlos Morales agreed to allow U.S. troops to take over the operation of customs houses, where goods arriving in the Dominican Republic were taxed. The United States took over repayment of the nation's debts and gave the Dominican government 45 percent of the customs taxes, which turned out to be considerably more than they had been able to collect themselves.

In 1914, an election was scheduled, but the winner soon resigned, asking the United States to help settle the violence that erupted. U.S. occupation began in 1916, with a military governor and U.S. troops in control until 1922. The last U.S. troops left in 1924.

Rafael Trujillo as a young man in military uniform

Mixed feelings surrounded these times. The U.S. occupation not only stabilized the unrest but also balanced the budget and brought in high revenues from sugar and other exports. Sanitation facilities were greatly improved. Schools and hospitals were built and their staffs were trained. Instead of each political party having its own army, a National Guard was established. However, many people opposed import taxes and resented civil rights issues such as censorship and the U.S. servicemen's treatment of Dominicans. By 1920, the nation was close to rebellion.

The occupation was not popular in the United States, either. In 1922, the Dominican Republic held its own elections, and within two years, the last of the U.S. troops had left. Meanwhile, a young man named Rafael Leonidas Trujillo Molina was working his way up through the ranks of the military. President Horacio Vásquez was elected in the free elections of 1924. The economy improved and Santo Domingo was modernized in this stable period. The young Trujillo continued his climb and became commander of the National Army.

The Trujillo Years

In February 1930, Rafael Trujillo became dictator through rigged elections and stayed in control until 1961. Through good public relations, his popularity soared abroad and among many Dominicans until the 1950s. Controversy still surrounds Trujillo's rule, both internationally and among Dominicans. Although few people question the fact that Trujillo's personal greed for power and wealth led to many questionable actions, even today some residents regard him as a stern but kind father figure.

During his first year in office, Congress named Trujillo "highest general" and "Benefactor of the Fatherland." His image was helped by a devastating hurricane in September 1930, one of the worst the island had ever suffered. This gave him the chance to rebuild the capital city and show the people what he could do for them. Almost everyone thought that he was an ideal leader. Behind the scenes, however, Trujillo was gaining more and more power. He took control of the Congress and other government branches, as well as many private organizations. Even the Catholic Church worked within his guidelines.

Trujillo succeeded in stabilizing the national currency and finally paid off all foreign debt. A middle class began to emerge, and education was at an all-time high with more than three times more schools. He expanded Dominican industry and

One Man's Ego

After his "election," Trujillo renamed Santo Domingo *Ciudad Trujillo* (Trujillo City). Across the country, large posters and billboards were put up, with the words "God and Trujillo" in big letters. Statues and portraits of the dictator were displayed everywhere. His followers rewrote the nation's history to glorify him. In the many schools he built and funded, subject matter seldom strayed from exaggerated praise of Trujillo.

built roads, railways, airports, and seaports. His efforts to increase living standards and provide the needy with public welfare improved the lives of many Dominicans. Farming techniques were improved and livestock production increased dramatically, while the mining industry saw its best time in years. Statistically, this was a golden era, but there was a darker side.

Any serious threats to Trujillo's career were disposed of by his faithful army. Strange accidents and abrupt suicides scarred the shiny exterior of his government. From time to time he allowed elections, where very minor opponents offered no real threat. From 1938 to 1942, he used his brother Héctor and other trusted associates as "puppets" in the office of president. Trujillo continued to hold all the power. He pulled the strings on his puppet presidents and the military eliminated anyone who opposed him.

In 1937, just two years after the border settlement between the two countries, Trujillo ordered the brutal massacre of up to 20,000 Haitians living in the Dominican Republic. Through bribed cover-ups, his public image remained favorable even after this.

For the average Dominican, some aspects of daily life improved under Trujillo's rigid control, although citizens had few freedoms. Crime was punished brutally, and opposition of any sort was not tolerated.

Shipping and port facilities on the Ozama River in Santo Domingo

Family Fortunes

Trujillo's family began to build up a fortune based on sugar, land, and anything he desired. Trujillo forced small farmers off their land and built plantations for his family members at government expense. By the end of his rule, his family controlled more than 60 percent of the nation's agriculture and industry. In effect, they owned the country, including twelve of its fifteen sugar mills.

In 1960, when Trujillo tried to have the president of Venezuela assassinated because he denounced Trujillo's dictatorship, the world began to realize what was really going on in the Dominican Republic. The Organization of American States (OAS) banned the Dominican Republic, and the United States broke off all relations. In 1961, even the Catholic Church denounced Trujillo. On May 30, 1961, Rafael Trujillo was ambushed and killed. The press suggested that the U.S. Central Intelligence Agency had supplied the weapons.

Joaquín Balaguer, the former president of the Dominican Republic, at his office in the Palacio Nacional, Santo Domingo

The Struggle for Self-Government

President Joaquín Balaguer, Trujillo's puppet, was suddenly in charge following the assassination. He quickly renounced the former dictator and began to relax many of Trujillo's stricter policies. He successfully prevented the Trujillo family from regaining power and finally exiled them. In January 1962, Balaguer was ousted in a coup—a rebellious uprising.

December 20, 1962, was the day of the first free election in the Dominican Republic. Juan Bosch Gaviño of the

Dominican Revolutionary Party (PRD) won, and focused mainly on economic and social reforms. He helped draw up the Constitution of 1963, which separated church and state, gave civilians control over the military, and restored many civil rights. The OAS lifted its ban.

The power struggle had not ended, however, and in 1963 the military overthrew the new president. The country remained a military state until 1965, when the PRD and loyal

Juan Bosch (left) visits with President John F. Kennedy in his White House office.

military officers organized a rebellion. Once again, the United States moved in to protect its own interests. President Lyndon B. Johnson sent in 20,000 U.S. troops to support the government in ending the civil war, and the OAS endorsed the occupation.

The United States now had more to worry about than the island's political instability. This unrest also had an economic impact. After Trujillo's death, major American companies had invested more than $87 million in real estate in the Dominican Republic, and the corporate powers had no intention of letting a new dictator or communist government interfere. The OAS sent in peacekeepers, and in 1966 Balaguer was re-elected.

Under this supervised government, Balaguer made many reforms. During three terms, he often appointed members of the opposing party to government positions, something new in the Dominican Republic. He also restricted military power and prevented the army from interfering in government. Businesses became more profitable, and the government began to help rural people who lived in poverty. But, like his teacher Trujillo, Balaguer used the national police to deal with anyone who opposed him.

In the elections of 1978, PRD member Antonio Guzmán Fernández gained power but was unsuccessful with reforms. However, he and his successor, Salvador Jorge Blanco, managed to reduce inflation from 38 to 14 percent and to establish a tradition of free elections. Balaguer won again in 1986 with 41.6 percent of the vote. He remained in power nearly twenty-eight years, until he was 87 years old. However, many people believed his 1994 re-election was rigged, and he was forced to step down in 1996.

The progressive leader Leonel Fernández Reyna was elected president with an absolute majority of more than half the votes cast in a 1996 special election. His administration has been especially strong in its foreign policy, trying to globalize the Dominican economy by working actively with the United States and other countries to increase trade.

Opposite: **U.S. paratroopers are greeted with anti-American slogans as they patrol Santo Domingo in 1965.**

Finally, Democracy

A FTER YEARS OF DICTATORSHIP AND TURMOIL, TODAY'S government tries to maintain a balance between the rights of the people and the need to make society run smoothly. Dominicans now elect their officials, but some would still feel more comfortable with more governmental control. And the people in power often got there because of who they know— their political connections.

Opposite: **The National Palace, or *Palacio Nacional*, the Dominican Republic's capitol**

The president acts as chief of state, with an appointed cabinet, usually made up of 15 secretaries. The legislature is composed of a 30-member Senate, with a 149-member Chamber of Deputies. The legislature and president are elected directly by voters who are at least eighteen years old. Members of the military and the police force, and prisoners, may not vote.

President Leonel Fernández Reyna of the Dominican Republic (left) visits with President René Préval (right) of Haiti.

The government is divided into twenty-nine provinces and one national district, which includes the capital city of Santo Domingo. Each Senate member represents a province

Provinces

1 Azua	11 Independencia	21 Puerto Plata
2 Bahoruco	12 La Altagracia	22 Salcedo
3 Barahona	13 La Romana	23 Samaná
4 Dajabón	14 La Vega	24 Sánchez Ramírez
5 Distrito Nacional	15 María Trinidad Sánchez	25 San Cristóbal
6 Duarte	16 Monseñor Nouel	26 San Juan
7 Elías Piña	17 Monte Cristi	27 San Pedro de Macorís
8 El Seibo	18 Monte Plata	28 Santiago
9 Espaillat	19 Pedernales	29 Santiago Rodríguez
10 Hato Mayor	20 Peravia	30 Valverde

and each province has its own governor, who is appointed by the president. The president also appoints the leaders of each county, called a commune. Each commune is then divided into townships. There are a total of 115 townships in the nation. Their leaders are elected directly by the people.

Dividing the Power

The Dominican constitution allows the president to appoint all the major members of the government. In this way, he may surround himself with people of the same party, who will then want to please the man who can reappoint them. Until recently, political power was also stacked in the president's favor at the voting polls because voters could choose only the members of one party or the other. But today, voters can evaluate each candidate and skip

A Flag for the Government, a Flag for Children

The national flag of the Dominican Republic is red, white, and blue, with the Dominican coat of arms in the center. This is the flag flown by the government. For annual Independence Day celebrations, children make simple flags that do not include the coat of arms. The colors and symbols used in the flag symbolize patriotism and national pride. The blue sections of the flag represent liberty, while the red sections stand for the blood of the heroes who died to preserve it. The white section, in the shape of a cross dividing the red and blue, is a symbol of salvation.

Left: **Dominicans cast their votes at a local school in the Villa Duarte section of Santo Domingo.**

Right: **1996 presidential election posters**

back and forth between parties to vote for individuals, so the Congress no longer has to be the same party as the president.

One of the most influential political parties is the Dominican Revolutionary Party (PRD). Established in 1939, the PRD has a liberal philosophy. Juan Bosch, former president and PRD member, later formed the Dominican Liberation Party (PLD), which is considered even more liberal. These parties focus on helping the poor and the working people. Both of these groups have humanitarian philosophies.

Long-time president Joaquín Balaguer was a member of the conservative Reformist Party (PR). In 1985, another conservative group called the Revolutionary Social Christian Party (PRSC) formed. To gain power, this party and the PR combined forces to create the Social Christian Reformist Party (PRSC). The PRSC, the PLD, and the PRD are now the three major political groups in the Dominican Republic.

Elected to a four-year term, the president is in charge of all diplomatic relations and can veto bills passed by Congress. As

How People Vote

There is no tradition of free elections in the Dominican Republic, and it will take many years before everyone begins to have real faith in the process. Some uneducated people may vote the way their employers tell them to, thinking that the employers know what is best for the economy and, therefore, for their jobs. Some voters also believe that their votes are not secret, and that they will be punished for not voting as they are told. But things are slowly changing as people begin to trust the system.

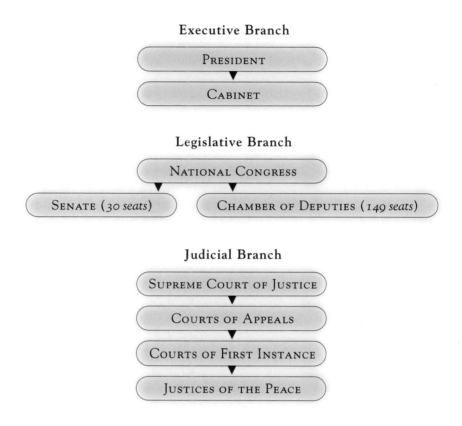

Executive Branch

PRESIDENT
▼
CABINET

Legislative Branch

NATIONAL CONGRESS
▼   ▼
SENATE (30 seats)   CHAMBER OF DEPUTIES (149 seats)

Judicial Branch

SUPREME COURT OF JUSTICE
▼
COURTS OF APPEALS
▼
COURTS OF FIRST INSTANCE
▼
JUSTICES OF THE PEACE

commander of the armed forces, the president is in charge of military appointments and sending out troops. Perhaps his greatest power is his ability to take charge in a state of emergency. During a state of emergency, all basic civil rights are suspended. The president then may do whatever he feels is necessary.

The Senate and the Chamber of Deputies, together called the Congress, form the legislative branch. Only this branch can declare a state of emergency. They are also in charge of taxes, immigration, political divisions, and other legal matters. Congress is also responsible for controlling the power of the president. They give him an annual review and decide to approve or reject presidential proposals. Representatives in Congress are elected by locality. Each province and the national district send one senator (for a total of 30). The 149 members of the Chamber of Deputies are chosen according to the population of their area. The U.S. Senate and House of Representatives are elected in the same way.

At the top of the judicial branch of government is the Supreme Court, with at least nine members. This court decides cases concerning the president and all other government officials, including congressional members. Unlike the U.S. Supreme Court justices, who are appointed for life, Dominican judges are appointed every four years, after the election of a new government. This makes their decisions subject to the political mood of the moment, since the president controls their reappointment to office. Although they are officially appointed by the legislative branch, the president usually controls the Congress. Despite this, since the 1960s, the court has become more independent, even if it is still not an equal branch of government.

Unfortunately, many people want to get these government positions so that they can obtain bribes. Most government employees regularly supplement their incomes with bribe money, and each time salaries are cut, the corruption in government grows. Also, government contracts are awarded to businesses in return for money paid directly to the official who makes the decision. Money may also be paid to a lower-ranking government employee who arranges an introduction to the right official.

President Leonel Fernández Reyna

Leonel Fernández Reyna was born in 1953 in Santo Domingo. He studied in New York and at the university in Santo Domingo. He earned a doctorate degree in 1978, with top honors in law. Before being elected president in 1996, Fernandez served as secretary of international affairs for the Dominican Liberation Party (PLD), and in 1994 he was a candidate for vice president.

Santo Domingo: Did You Know This?

Population: 2,411,895.

Founded: 1496 by Bartholomew Columbus.

Previous names: Founded as *Nueva Isabela*. From 1936 to 1961, the city was renamed *Ciudad Trujillo*.

Santo Domingo lies at the mouth of the Ozama River, which empties into the Caribbean Sea on the southern coast. The *Museo de las Casas Reales* (Museum of the Royal Houses) has exhibits on Columbus's journeys and Spanish Caribbean history.

Many of the city's historical sites and neighborhoods were restored during the 1970s to allow visitors to experience the rich history of Santo Domingo. Today, it is a rapidly growing city that houses many middle-class Dominicans as well as a large population of impoverished country people, or *campesinos*, who have come to find work. In addition to housing shortages, the rising population has put excessive stress on the electric and water supplies, making blackouts and poor sanitation a serious problem. Since 1950, Santo Domingo has had more rural people move in than any other city in the world.

Santo Domingo claims several "New World firsts," including:

- Oldest surviving European city in the Western Hemisphere.
- First permanent (and first Spanish) colony in the New World.
- Alcázar de Colón, the first European fortress in the Americas, dating back to the early 1500s.
- The Cathedral of Santa María la Menor, completed in 1540, the oldest church in the West Indies.
- The University of Santo Domingo, the first university founded in the New World.

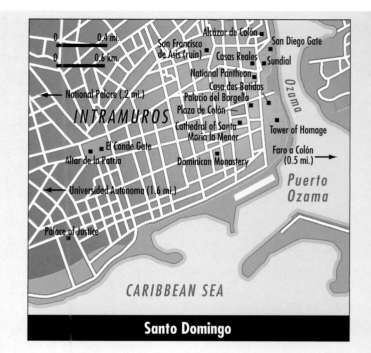

Santo Domingo

The Constitution

The Dominican Republic has had several different constitutions, each reflecting the political mood of the time—or at least the thinking of the current president. The latest one was adopted in 1966 after the civil war that followed Trujillo's rule, and was modified in 1994. While the constitution of 1966 puts few limitations on the president's powers, it stresses civil rights and give Dominicans liberties they had never been guaranteed before.

In 1978, reforms were made to the constitution to reduce the military's political involvement. It was feared that a military too close to the government might plan another coup. The changes also gave the military more civic duties. The armed forces are now responsible for building roads, building and staffing medical and educational facilities, and even building houses and replanting forests.

The Military

The armed forces are made up of three branches—the army, the air force, and the navy. During times of political trouble in Haiti, the Dominican Republic views its neighbor as a potential danger. The military is also responsible for helping the national police keep order inside the Dominican Republic. Although they still have some potential for seizing political power, the Dominican military is much smaller than that of most Latin American countries—only one-tenth of 1 percent of the adult population.

The National Anthem

The Dominican National Anthem is *Himno Nacional de la República Dominicana*, and its first line begins "Valiant Quisqueyans, let's raise our voices. . . ." *Quisqueya* was the Taíno name for the eastern side of the island, and Dominicans use this as a fond nickname for their country. It gives them a romantic tie with their past, though there is probably very little Indian blood in any Dominican today.

A ceremonial guard at the Columbus Lighthouse, or *Faro a Colón*

CHAPTER SIX

Money Matters: From Sugar to Tourism

Throughout its history, the Dominican Republic's financial state has been a roller coaster of success and failure. It was not until the middle of the twentieth century that foreign debts were finally paid off and the nation could focus on its internal problems. Exports of agricultural goods, especially sugar, and mining products contribute to the nation's income. Tourism is a growing source of income today, because of the island's long stretches of beautiful beaches. There is a growing middle class, but poverty continues to plague a large percentage of the population.

Tourists meeting outside a Dominican gift shop

The economic interests of the Dominican Republic are primarily in four areas. Agriculture provides money from exports as well as food for the people. Mining brings in foreign trade as well. Factories primarily manufacture products sold within the

The Dominican labor force

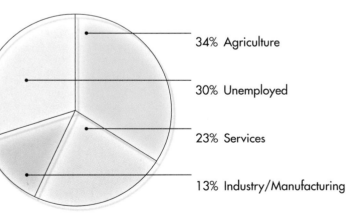

34% Agriculture

30% Unemployed

23% Services

13% Industry/Manufacturing

Who Owns What?

A good way to understand how narrowly wealth is distributed in the Dominican Republic is to look at the ownership of items that many people in the United States and Canada take for granted. For example, few of the island's residents own a car. One in six people owns a radio, while only one in eleven owns a TV set. TV owners have many friends and neighbors who gather to watch local and cable programs. One in every fourteen households has a telephone.

Aerial view of La Romana sugar mill along the Dulce River

country, except goods made in tax-free zones operated by foreign companies. Finally, tourism is a booming industry that has contributed significantly to the economy and is still rising in importance.

Because the agricultural industry provides not only cash from exports, but also necessary food for islanders, it is not surprising that many people work as farmers. Nearly 85 percent of these farmers own small plots of less than 50 acres (20 ha). These small farms, however, make up only 12 percent of the total farmland. Others, mostly small farmers called *campesinos*, own a few *tareas* of land (less than one-sixth of an acre). The rest of the farmland is owned by the government or large companies, mostly to grow sugarcane.

Sweet Success

Altogether, 592,800 acres (239,906 ha) are devoted to growing sugar, most of it on the southern and eastern coasts. The State Sugar Council (CEA) is the largest sugarcane producer. It was established in 1966 when the government took over the large plantations owned by the Trujillo family. The two other

From the Fields to the Table

Sugar processing is a major industry in the Dominican Republic. It takes many steps to turn the thick, tough stalks of sugarcane into the fine white crystals of refined sugar. After the cane is harvested, the stalks are washed, shredded, and placed in a machine that sprays the strands of cane with water to dissolve the sugar. The resulting fluid is called cane juice. This juice is heated, and lime (calcium hydroxide) is added to clear out any impurities. The solution is then infused with carbon dioxide to get rid of the excess lime. The liquid is then poured into big tanks where it evaporates and becomes a syrup.

The syrup is transferred to large vacuum pans where it boils at a lower temperature so that it doesn't burn. Once sugar crystals have formed, they are removed by a machine called a centrifuge, which spins the syrup until all the crystals separate. These crystals are known as raw sugar. To make pure white sugar, the raw sugar is rinsed and dissolved again. It is filtered many times until it is totally clear. This solution is then evaporated, separated in the centrifuge, and dried in large drying drums. The result is white sugar, ready to fill the sugar bowl.

Haitian sugarcane workers live in rundown shacks and work under hazardous conditions.

major producers are Central Romana and the family-owned Casa Viccini. Private sugarcane farmers sell their crops directly to mills, where it is processed into sugar.

Working conditions on the major sugarcane farms are dreadful. Most Dominicans are too proud to "lower" themselves to working for low wages in the cane fields. As a result, companies hire Haitians to work in the fields. The Haitians work nonstop for twelve to fifteen hours a day, and the workers are as young as eight years old. They are provided with minimum shelter—rundown shacks called *bateyes*. There are no cooking or sanitary facilities, and no running water. Even so, many Haitians find the working conditions better than those in their own country. These Haitian communities are most often found on the large plantations.

Annually, the industry processes 1 million short tons (910,000 metric tons) of sugar cane. Three-quarters of the crop is exported to the United States. In addition to sugar itself, molasses and rum are manufactured and sold, increasing profits for the sugarcane industry.

Sugar is not the only major crop, however. Tobacco, dating back to the Taíno, has always been important, grown primarily for cigars. After a high-priced market year in 1979, the 1980s brought low prices and a devastating set of crop diseases that have seriously hurt this industry. It is now slowly coming back as foreign cigar companies have begun to invest.

The Dominican Republic also exports products such as cocoa, coffee, ornamental plants, and what are known as "winter vegetables." Winter vegetables are crops that cannot be grown during the winter in the United States and Canada. Thanks to farms in the Dominican Republic and elsewhere, grocery stores in Boston and Toronto offer a variety of citrus and tropical fruits all winter, at more reasonable prices than indoor-grown local fruits. And because of the Caribbean Basin Initiative (CBI), the market runs smoothly. More than 3,000 products may be imported to the United States free of duties—taxes charged on imported products.

Men wetting dark tobacco seedlings

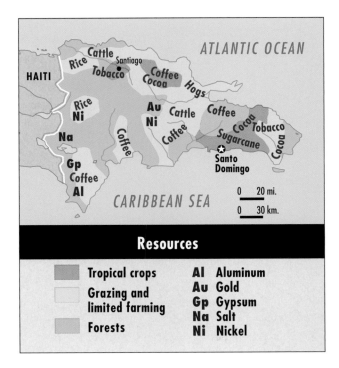

Resources

▨ Tropical crops	**Al** Aluminum
▢ Grazing and limited farming	**Au** Gold
	Gp Gypsum
▨ Forests	**Na** Salt
	Ni Nickel

Popular fruits and other foods are sold at the markets.

Many other crops are grown primarily for the Dominicans, including rice, beans, plantains, and cassava, a plant used for making tapioca. Corn, bananas, peanuts, tomatoes, lettuce, and cabbage are also staple food crops. Popular fruits grown year-round are avocados, mangoes, guavas, passion fruit, tamarinds, and coconuts. Seasonings such as scallions, coriander, onions, and garlic are found all over the island. One of the few agricultural products the Dominican Republic imports is rice, although it does grow some of its own.

In the eastern sections of the country, beef cattle are raised on large ranches. Most of this beef is exported, with 10 percent going to the United States. Small farms produce pork, chicken, and other meats used for domestic consumption. Due to bans on cutting trees, most of the nation's wood products are now imported, totaling $30 million a year. Most imported products come from the United States and Japan.

Centavos from Heaven

The national currency is the Dominican Republic peso. The peso is divided into 100 centavos. Paper bills are available in denominations of 1,000, 500, 50, 20, 10, and 5 pesos. Coins come in 1 peso and 50, 25, 10, 5, and 1 centavos. The paper bills have images of important political figures on the front, including Ramón Matías Mella, Francisco del Rosario Sánchez, and Juan Pablo Duarte. Significant landmarks are pictured on the back. Structures such as the *Presas Hidroelétricas y de Riego*, a hydro-electric dam, are also shown to stress the importance of electric power and water for irrigation and consumption.

The peso's value compared to other major world currencies has declined in recent years. This benefits the country in one way—the more valuable the foreign currency, the more tourists will be attracted to the Dominican Republic, and the more they will spend once they get there. In 1999, U.S.$1 was equal to 15.75 pesos, and Canadian $1 equaled 10.43 pesos.

Since Europeans found gold here five centuries ago, mining has become an important asset to the economy. The Dominican Republic still has gold as well as silver. The alloy, or mixture, of gold and silver, called *doré*, is the form in which these metals are often sold. Among the other important metals mined are ferronickel, copper, iron, bauxite, and mercury. The central region of the country has nickel mines, which produce about 33,000 tons (30,000 metric tons) a year.

What the Dominican Republic Grows, Makes and Mines

Agriculture (1995; in Dominican pesos)

Coffee	2,067,000,000
Rice	1,781,000,000
Sugarcane	1,586,000,000
Chicken meat	1,692,000,000

Manufacturing (1995–1996)

Cement	1,551,000 metric tons
Refined sugar	109,900 metric tons
Beer	2,010,000 hectoliters

Mining (1998)

Nickel	30,400 metric tons
Gold	122,501 troy ounces

A rum warehouse in Santiago

Compared to agriculture and mining, manufacturing brings in a small part of the nation's income. Most of what is produced by privately owned factories stays in the country. Molasses, sugar, and rum make up nearly all the export manufacturing. Fifty percent of the manufacturing is food and beverage processing. The remainder includes textiles, chemicals, pharmaceuticals, and cement. Eighteen percent of the labor force is employed by the manufacturing industry, an increase of nearly 10 percent in the past twenty years.

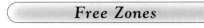

Free Zones

Much of the nation's industrial work occurs in the free zones. These are foreign-owned areas where no tariffs, or taxes on imported goods, are charged on products made. Usually, free zones are full of factories and plants that turn raw materials into finished products. The Dominican government supplies the buildings in order to encourage corporations to move there. Low wages, an available workforce, and low taxes make these zones attractive to foreign businesses. There are twenty-four free zones in the Dominican Republic, the world's fourth-largest location for such zones.

A young woman working at a garment factory in a free zone

Two-thirds of these zones are owned by U.S.-based companies, but Italy, Liberia, Taiwan, and Hong Kong also own land in these zones. The majority of free-zone workers are women who are paid next to nothing and receive no benefits. In 1990, the average monthly salary for a free-zone worker was equivalent to U.S.$59. Most of the jobs consist of assembly and factory work, resulting in almost 200,000 jobs for unskilled workers during peak periods. Most of the products—electronics, jewelry, furniture, clothing, and shoes—are exported.

Free zones have not only created much-needed jobs but also have brought more advanced technology to the island. The companies contribute to the local economy through their rent payments and purchases of utilities and supplies needed for production. The free zones are an unstable source of income, however, because most companies would move quickly if they found a better deal somewhere else.

Technology and Tourism

Technology on the island is somewhat more advanced than it is in many other Caribbean islands and Latin American countries. The Dominican Republic is first among this group in telecommunications and has widespread fiberoptics telephone networks. This technology, however, is mostly limited to city areas. This small country now has four international airports, part of the strong effort to increase tourism.

Getting Around

How do the people get around without cars? They rarely use trains, because the railway systems are mainly used to move freight, not passengers. In fact, none of the nation's many train lines connect to Santo Domingo, and most do not even connect to one another. And the inexpensive buses that run in urban areas are unpleasantly crowded.

Bicycles are very common, and mopeds and motorcycles have recently become very popular. A unique taxi system helps solve the day-to-day transportation needs. Privately owned taxicabs, many of which look as though they might break down at any minute, stop to pick up passengers beside the roads. More and more passengers crowd in, each paying a few pesos, until the cabs are overflowing, often with passengers sitting on the fenders. These informal "buses" carry thousands of Dominicans each day. Taxis similar to those in the United States and Canada operate in the cities.

Dominicans and tourists relaxing at Sosúa Beach

Its beautiful beaches and sunny weather make this island a dream vacation spot. The Dominicans are well known for their friendliness, based on their good nature and encouraged by their wish to increase tourism. With 2 million tourists a year, half of the national foreign earnings come from this industry. Twenty percent of these tourists are from the United States (in the 1980s, this figure was nearly 50 percent). Interestingly, the need for a good public image to encourage tourism has helped create a more stable political climate. Dominicans realize that tourists will not visit a place that is having riots and revolutions.

The peak tourist season is mid-December through mid-April, reflecting the worst weather conditions in Europe and North America rather than the best seasons on the island. During the off-season, the number of tourists—and the prices for tourist services—drop drastically. A great deal of tourist money goes to the many foreign-owned resorts along the coast, but many visitors prefer a more authentic experience and explore the countryside and Santo Domingo, contributing directly to the local economy.

In 1971, the government passed the Tourist Incentive Law to improve the cleanliness of the water supply and availability of electricity. These issues affect tourism, because no one wants to spend a vacation sick, or in a dark hotel room. Many improvements have been made since the law was passed, but naturally the tourist areas have seen the most change.

Blackout!

All island residents are more than familiar with *apagones* (blackouts). This term comes from the Spanish verb *apagar*, which means "to turn out a light." These blackouts can last for a few hours or a few days, causing many problems. Refrigeration is cut off and business comes to a standstill. During blackouts in Santo Domingo, every building loses power except the *Faro a Colón*. A monument to Christopher Columbus, it continues to send a brilliant light into the night sky, forming a cross over the dark city.

Each year, many parts of the Dominican Republic endure at least 500 hours of power outages. That is equal to 20 full days and nights without electricity. The high fuel prices and the inability to meet power demands has slowed the growth of technology across the island. Even now, only half of the nation's homes have electricity.

The shortage of housing is a major crisis that faces thousands of Dominicans each day. As the cities fill up with rural families looking for work, the streets fill up with makeshift shelters made out of boxes or whatever is available. Even for those who find housing, life is a struggle with little or no sanitation, no running water, and no cooking facilities. Matters finally got so bad in 1995 that many residents of these shantytowns took over the churches, refusing to leave until something was done. Many of the protesters had homes to go to, but sleeping on a hard pew was preferable to the unsanitary conditions they faced in their rundown houses.

The government ignored this, and instead sent troops into the *barrios* (poor neighborhoods) to be sure that no one tried to make improvements on their homes. The government said that major city reconstruction would soon take place in these *barrios*. However, most of these new building projects involved tearing down the barely livable homes to build monuments and attractions that would look good for the city. Their poverty was ignored, and the former residents were left homeless.

A study conducted by the Pontifical Catholic University *Madre y Maestra* in Santiago projected dismal estimates on housing. They found that in order to have enough housing for all of the poor in the Dominican Republic, 6,542 houses would need to be built each month for ten years! Other church groups pointed out the unequal distribution of land in relation to wealth—more than 70 percent of the land-owning population had plots less than 1 acre (0.4 ha) in size.

Run-down houses along the Ozama River are a result of the shortage of housing.

La Gente

L A GENTE IS THE SPANISH TERM FOR NOT ONLY "THE PEOPLE," but also "the nation" and "the family." The multiple meanings of this term reflect the spirit of the people—one nation, one family.

In 1998, the population of this small country was estimated at 8,217,000. The average 2 percent annual population growth means that there will be nearly 9 million people living in the Dominican Republic by the year 2003. The population density is 437 people per square mile (169 per sq km), with 59 percent in urban areas, and 41 percent in rural zones. This might seem to be a fairly even distribution, except that there are only two large urban areas in the country. So more than half the population is packed into two major cities.

Medical care in the Dominican Republic is relatively poor, with about 1,052 people to each doctor and 838 people to each hospital bed. Despite these conditions, the average life

Opposite: **A rainy day in the Cibao region**

Population density of the Dominican Republic

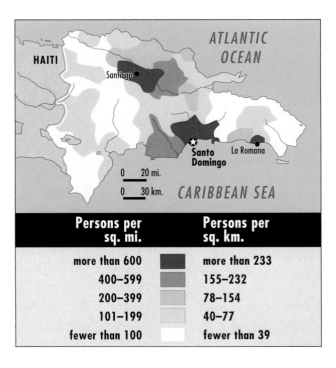

Persons per sq. mi.		Persons per sq. km.
more than 600		more than 233
400–599		155–232
200–399		78–154
101–199		40–77
fewer than 100		fewer than 39

A medical clinic in the Dominican Republic

expectancy is sixty-seven for men and seventy-two for women.

Laws require all children between seven and fourteen years old to attend school, but only 70 percent of these children actually attend classes. Schools are crowded and understaffed, and many children are unable to continue their education past the eighth grade. Despite the low attendance rate at schools, however, 82 percent of the people can read and write. This is impressive compared to neighboring Haiti's 45 percent literacy.

The Dominican Republic has twenty-eight universities. The cost of a college education in the Dominican Republic varies, and universities offer student loans that can be repaid after graduation. Some students go to Europe or the United States to attend college preparatory schools and universities.

Children congregate in a schoolyard of the Samaná Peninsula.

In any nation of people with mixed ethnic backgrounds, racism and discrimination sometimes become problems. Although most Dominicans claim that there is no racism, some attitudes cannot be ignored. Dominicans separate races into four categories. *Blanco* is the term for a person who is completely Caucasian (of European ancestry)—and usually also a member of the upper class. *Indio claro* and *indio oscuro* are terms that describe mulattoes (people of mixed African and European ancestry), with the first group being "whiter," and the second group mostly black. The term *negro*, which is the Spanish word for "black," refers to people of pure African descent and is usually reserved for Haitians.

As a result of years of European domination, many residents do not acknowledge their African roots. This is why the term "*indio*" is used in describing mulattoes. Although there were no Taíno survivors, many claim this is where their dark skin came from. Many leaders, including Rafael Trujillo, a mulatto, filled the media with anti-African propaganda for years. His henchmen actually rewrote Dominican history, claiming the existence of "*Hispanidad.*" According to *Hispanidad*, the island's people are "the most Spanish people of America"; in other words, the most white.

Who Lives in the Dominican Republic?

Mulatto (mixed African and European)	73%
European	16%
African	11%

Women of mixed ethnic backgrounds marching in the Easter Holy Week procession

Trujillo's Racism

The dictator Rafael Trujillo went as far as to wear makeup in public to lighten his skin. He directed his racism at the Haitians, claiming that their immigration into the Dominican Republic would "darken" the country. Border patrols were told to have any suspects pronounce *perejil*, the Spanish word for "parsley." In the Haitian Creole language, the letter *r* is pronounced like a *w*, and there is no letter *j*. Any person who could not pronounce the word correctly was imprisoned.

The Bottom Rung

The social class structure is influenced by racial and economic issues, as well as by family legacy. The largest group is the lower class. One-quarter of these people are unemployed. Although they are paid at a lower rate, poor women tend to find jobs more easily than the men, especially in rural areas. As a result, women actually average a higher income and often support their households. But most families don't make enough to meet their needs, and poverty is widespread.

A produce vendor, or *marchanta,* in Puerto Plata

The rural lower class is made up of small landowners and migrant laborers. Those who move to the city to find work are often disappointed. They find no housing, no electricity, and no sanitation—far from the promising future they had hoped for. These migrants keep their ties with their rural relatives and help one another in times of need. They call this tie a *cadena*, which means "chain."

The black people, especially the Haitians, are at the bottom of the social ladder. Before a 1990 law banned the custom, agents were sent to Haiti to recruit workers for the cane plantations. More than 200,000 Haitians live in the Dominican Republic, and they are not welcomed by the residents. Most of these people work in the sugarcane fields and live in less than humane conditions for very little pay. The discrimination against this population is directly linked to anti-African feelings.

A new middle- to upper-class development in Puerto Plata

Breaking Through

In recent years, the middle class has begun to grow in the Dominican Republic. Today, this group makes up nearly one-third of the population. The middle class is most affected by national economic changes, especially in the sugar and tourism industries. And middle class people are increasingly influential under the present government.

La Gente Fina

La gente fina (the refined people) is how the rich are described. This term reflects the idea that money influences a person's worth. Although the rich are few in number and do not have the huge plantations they once did, they are still very influential. Bankers and businesspeople are now at the top of the economic ladder, but strong family ties still have the greatest influence on social standing.

In the cities, the upper classes are divided into "new" and "old" money. *La gente de primera* (the first class) is made up of the old families with generations of money. Their kinship ties are strong, and family matters are often their main interest. The "new" money families are people who have succeeded in business and professions. The upper classes are most concerned with international issues and the future of their country, as are most educated Dominicans.

Journey to the Future

Because of economic and social restraints at home, many Dominicans leave the country to find a better way of life. Many emigrate to find jobs, sending money back to support their families. Others join relatives already living in other countries. Education and job opportunities are major reasons for leaving the island, and it is usually those who are better off who make the journey. Although some countries issue a certain number of visas each year for immigrants, illegal entry into the United States and other countries is very common.

Opposite: **The Dominican Day Parade in New York City**

VIRGEN DE LA ALTAGRACIA

Spanish Pronunciation

In Spanish, the way words are pronounced is almost as important as the words themselves. The following guide shows how each letter is pronounced in Spanish, with word examples in English and in Spanish. The Spanish words are followed by their English translation.

Try pronouncing the words out loud in English, and then in Spanish. If you pronounce an English word according to the Spanish guidelines, you'll have a Spanish accent!

Letter	English Example	Spanish Example and (Translation)	Description
a	father	papa (potato)	
b	Bob	boca (mouth)	at the beginning of a word
	—	cabo (end)	between vowels, close to "v"
c	cat	copo (snowflake)	before a, o, or u, like "k"
	ceiling	cena (supper)	before e or i, like "s"
ch	change	chiste (joke)	
d	date	dato (fact)	at the beginning of a word
		cada (each)	between vowels, like "th" in "the"
e	they	leche (milk)	
f	fat	fácil (easy)	
g	—	gente (people)	before e & i, like "h" of "ha!"
	game	gato (cat)	before a, o, or u, hard "g"
	guard	guiso (stew)	with u before e or i, hard "g"
h	—	hombre (man)	always silent

The United States is a popular destination for Dominican emigrants, especially New York City. Dominicans make up the second largest group of Hispanics in that city after Puerto Ricans, and Dominican neighborhoods are common in other

Letter	English Example	Spanish Example and (Translation)	Description
i	machine	piso (ground)	
j	—	jarra (jug, pitcher)	"h," as in hat
k	kale	kilogramo (kilogram)	
l	lace	lindo (pretty)	
ll	—	llave (faucet or key)	like "y" in yes
m	mail	mundo (world)	
n	name	nada (nothing)	
ñ	—	niño (child)	like "ny" in canyon
o	rope	doña (madame)	
p	pole	poco (little)	
q	raquet	quince (fifteen)	
r	—	caro (expensive)	like "dd" in ladder
rr	—	perrito (puppy)	trilled (sound is rolled over the tongue)
s	song	sopa (soup)	
t	table	toro (bull)	
u	mute	luna (moon)	
v	—	vuelo (flight)	same as Spanish "b"
w	win	wat (watt)	rare in Spanish; used for English words
x	exit	éxito (success)	
		mixto	before consonant, like "s"
y	—	y (and)	like "i" in marine
	yet	yerno (son-in-law)	
z	—	zapato (shoe)	like "ss" in class

cities too. The number of visa applications increases by 25 percent each year, but only 20,000 persons are legally allowed entry into the United States. Some of the people who move illegally go through Puerto Rico. Passengers pay from

U.S.$1,000 to U.S.$2,000 for a plane from Saint Maarten, boat rides from there to St. Thomas and Puerto Rico, and a flight from there to the United States.

Most are not so fortunate, however, and they make the risky trip by boat across the Mona Passage—a dangerous stretch of water between the Dominican Republic and Puerto Rico. The Atlantic Ocean and the Caribbean Sea meet at this spot, creating strong currents and rough waters. Long, fifty-passenger boats called *yolas* cross the 90-mile (145-km) stretch of water, carefully trying not to be spotted by the U.S. Coast Guard. From Puerto Rico, many take a plane to the United States. Others work on Puerto Rico, where wages are considerably better than at home.

A Land of Voices

When the Europeans landed, they brought many things to the New World, including a language. Spanish is the official language of the Dominican Republic. It has been enriched by various African words, and many Taíno words found their way into the language as well. The Spanish you hear in the Dominican Republic is much softer than the dialects spoken in Mexico and South America. It is considered to be closest to the less-accented Castilian Spanish of Spain.

Some words used on the island were adopted from the Taíno language and survived because there were no Spanish words for things that were new to the Spanish. Plants like tobacco (*tabaco*) and cassava (*casabe*) kept their Taíno names, as did hammock (*hamaca*), canoes (*canoa*), and hurricanes

Traffic signs in Puerto Plata

(*huracán*). The word *cibao*, which means mountain, was also retained from the ancient language and is now used to describe major sections of the country.

African words, such as voodoo (or *vodú*) were also brought to the island and incorporated into daily use. The word for a hex or bad omen, *fucú*, came from an African language. The response to this hex is "*zafa*," another African word, which breaks the spell.

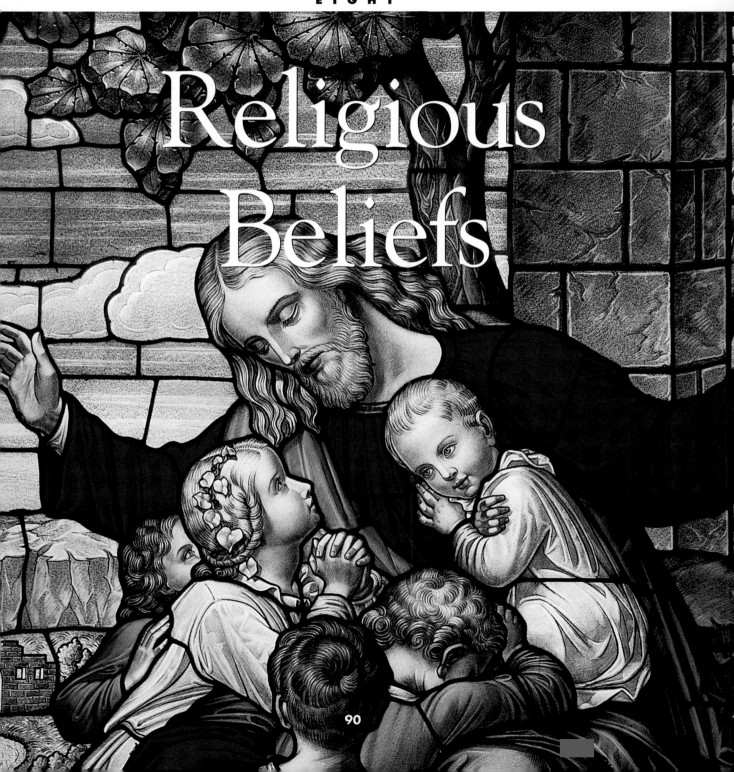

Religious Beliefs

Opposite: **Stained glass window of Jesus with children at the *Sagrado Corazón* church in the city of Moca**

THE CONSTITUTION OF THE DOMINICAN REPUBLIC GIVES ALL citizens freedom of religion. Although most of the country is Roman Catholic, Protestant and folk religions are also widespread. The small percentage of voodoo practitioners keep their beliefs to themselves, however, because voodoo, though legal, is socially frowned on and considered anti-Catholic.

Religions of the Dominican Republic*

Roman Catholic	95%
Protestant	2%
Jewish	.02%

*Does not equal 100%

Roman Catholics

More than 95 percent of the people in the Dominican Republic are Roman Catholic. This religion was brought to the island from Europe by the Spanish, who held the first Catholic mass in the New World in 1493. In 1540, the Cathedral of Santa María la Menor was completed in Santo Domingo. Six years later, the first archbishop of the islands was appointed.

Even today, many priests in the Dominican Republic come from Spain or were educated there. Priests are considered the most trusted of confidants, often serving not only as spiritual guides but also as political and

The *Basílica Catedral Nuestra Señora de la Encarnación* stands in the colonial area of the city of Santo Domingo.

social leaders. Many are highly involved with the problems of the poor, fighting to end poverty. The church also supplies teaching nuns for its many schools and colleges. A number of church-run training programs train teachers for public schools. Many nuns are nurses or run orphanages.

The priest-to-population ratio is very low—there are about 10,000 Catholics for every one priest. However, those in the upper ranks of the church—above the level of parish priest—are usually more interested in keeping the government happy. They prefer to stay out of social issues. The priests and nuns who work directly with the people are more concerned with the realities of community life. The shortage of priests and of money to fund projects is holding back their efforts, however.

Politically, the influence of the church has had an uneven history. Each government has given it varying degrees of importance, some ignoring it entirely and others using its influence over the people to their own advantage. In colonial days, the church was a major power in governing the island, but when the Spanish withdrew, the church lost much of its importance.

The church was most involved with politics during the rule of Trujillo, although officially it took no part. In 1954, Trujillo proclaimed Roman Catholicism the national religion and then used the church as another tool for controlling the people. For the most part, the church overlooked the darker side of Trujillo's politics until 1960. Finally, the religious leaders began to protest his treatment of those who opposed him.

Opposite: **A nun of Mother Teresa's order caring for a sick child**

Even the Pope Is Criticized

When the pope visited in 1992 to observe the 500th anniversary of Catholicism in the New World, the mass was celebrated at the Faro a Colón, an enormous monument built by the government to honor Columbus. During its construction, the monument cost taxpayers a lot of money, and entire neighborhoods of low-income housing were destroyed to make room for it. Many people felt it was wrong for the leader of the Catholic Church to honor this monument, which had cost so many poor people their homes. Many refused to attend the mass. But the church was in no position to argue with the government, which had decided that the mass would be held in their new showpiece monument.

In its attempts to build churches and help the communities across the island, the Catholic Church accepted a large amount of government funding, first from Trujillo and later from other presidents. Although the money is welcome, it makes it hard for the church to publicly oppose the government or its policies. This relationship between the church and state leaves one of the most influential groups in the country without a voice.

Religion is a major part of everyday life, so many of the nation's traditions are based on the Roman Catholic faith. Among these are large processions called *rosarios*. These paradelike gatherings are held in hopes of curing an illness or solving problems like drought or other natural disasters. The procession's leader carries a large rosary and an image of a saint, such as the Virgin Mary. Musicians follow, playing guitars, flutes, and assorted instruments. At the rear of the group are women, children, and the elderly. It is believed that all the members of the procession must complete the journey back to the starting point in order for the prayers to be answered.

As the *rosario* passes from town to town, the group stops at stations, also called *rosarios*. These are groups of crosses that represent the three crosses of Calvary. They are erected in rural areas as a meeting place for the processions and also as a symbol of welcome to any traveler. Processions such as these are more common in rural areas, where people follow the church traditions most faithfully.

Religious sites and statues are important symbols of faith for many Dominicans. One of these sacred shrines is the statue of Saint Anthony in Santo Domingo. It is said that the statue has the power to cause earthquakes if it is removed from its pedestal. Another important site is a statue of Christ named *Cristo de Bayaguana*. The most important shrine on the island is that of *Nuestra Señora de la*

A decorated float of Our Lady of Sorrow in *Semana Santa,* the Easter Holy Week procession

The *Basílica de Nuestra Señora de la Altagracia,* or Our Lady of the High Grace, in Higüey

Superstitions

Along with the beliefs taught by their church, many Dominicans also believe in some superstitions. Some of these are religious charms used to ward off sickness or evil, while others are mystical formulas. Called *oraciones,* these "rules" tell people how to avoid bad luck, and how to prevent troubles. Although you may find some of these superstitions strange, many people in the Dominican Republic and other countries believe strongly in them. Have you heard any of the following superstitions before?

- It is bad luck if a wedding guest wears black.
- If an unmarried woman agrees to be a godmother, she will never marry.
- If an unmarried woman is a bridesmaid three times, she will never marry.
- If a couple is wed in November, the marriage will not last.
- If a person sleeps with his or her feet pointed toward the front of the house, he or she will die.
- A statue or picture of a saint over the front door will keep evil from entering the house.

Altagracia (Our Lady of the Higher Grace) in Higüey. She is considered the island's protector, and the shrine is visited by many people each year.

Not all the shrines and statues are in public places, however. Almost every home, even those of the very poor, has a shrine. In a fine home, for example, a statue of the Virgin Mary may be placed on a lace cloth and decorated with a bouquet of fresh flowers. In the rundown shack of a poor farmer, a faded picture of a saint may be decorated with a ribbon.

Folk Traditions

Especially in rural areas, Roman Catholicism is combined with traditional folk religion. As well as following the beliefs of the church, the people find comfort in the spiritual and healing methods that have been passed down through generations. It is quite common for devout Catholics to consult a folk practitioner for spiritual advice or to prevent some calamity. One of the most respected folk practices is that of the *ensalmo*. This is a healing chant, usually performed by an elderly woman. Folk healers are called *curanderos*, and they work through the saints, asking special help for those in need. The witch doctors, called *brujos*, use herbs and other natural objects for healing. They are also believed to have the power to banish evil spirits.

Protestants

A very small percentage of Dominicans are Protestants. Among the major Protestant churches are the Protestant Episcopal Church and the Dominican Evangelical Church. Some of the smaller organizations include the Free Methodist Church, Seventh-Day Adventists, and the Assemblies of God.

Many Protestants are descendants of non-Spanish immigrants who came to the island in the early 1800s and brought their faith with them. Most of these churches stress the family and fundamentalism—a style of worship with less ceremony than the Catholic Church. In recent years, some of these fundamentalist faiths have converted increasing numbers of Dominicans. Despite differences in belief and opinion, there is no conflict between religious groups, nor has there been any religious persecution. Trujillo, however, expelled the Jehovah's Witnesses because they were politically neutral and he was unable to control them.

Market stall of merchandise for brujos and traditional healers

During World War II (1939–1945), when Jewish people in Germany and other European countries were persecuted by the Nazis, Trujillo opened his country to those who escaped. The small town of Sosúa was built by a group of European Jews, and it is still a center for the tiny Jewish population of the island. Santo Domingo has two synagogues. One is Orthodox and holds services in Hebrew and Yiddish; the other holds services in Hebrew and German.

Entrance to the synagogue founded by German Jewish refugees who escaped from the Holocaust and were given refuge at Sosúa in 1938

Voodoo

The rich ethnic mixture of the island has contributed to a unique religion called *voodoo*, which is found in different forms in several Caribbean countries. The Dominican form is called *gagá*. Voodoo is a mixture of influences from African, Native American, and Roman Catholic religions, but it is most influenced by the Dahomey region of Africa. The word *voodoo* means god, spirit, or sacred object. People who believe in voodoo worship one supreme being and many lesser spirits. They believe that each individual has a protector spirit who rewards that person with wealth and punishes with illness. Nature gods oversee the external world and are worshiped in seasonal celebrations. Family gods—the souls of dead ancestors—must be remembered with elaborate funerals and memorials, so that they will continue to protect the living.

The male priests of voodoo are called *hungans*; the females are called *mambos*. As well as serving as spiritual guides, the *mambos* and *hungans* can rid the human body of *loas*, or gods that possess the body. They also perform a divination ritual called *fa-a*. In this ritual, palm kernels are scattered on a cloth and the way they land is interpreted to predict the future and solve problems. The assistants to the priests and priestesses are called *laplas* and *onsi*, and the congregation is the *pitit kay*.

Voodoo is practiced most frequently along the Haitian border, and almost always in secret. It is socially unpopular because it is considered anti-Catholic and because it is associated with neighboring Haiti. People who practice it are looked down on. Voodoo products, however, can be found in markets throughout the island, probably more for the benefit of tourists than for island practitioners.

A Rich Blend of Cultures

THE DOMINICAN REPUBLIC'S rich history and mixed population have given the island a unique and lively culture. As groups of conquerors, slaves, and immigrants came to live there, they brought

along customs and arts that blended into the nation's way of life. Native Taíno foods, words, and medicines were adopted by the Spanish settlers, who also brought their own language, religion, and social customs. African slaves who were brought to the island carried in their hearts the religion of voodoo and the essential beat that inspired the merengue dance. Together with other contributions, these cultures mixed over time to make the lively island we know today.

Commuters using various modes of transportation during the morning rush

Marriage

In the Dominican Republic, young lovers may choose between a church wedding and a civil service. More than 80 percent decide on a civil marriage, called a free union, because it is much less expensive. Free unions are also popular because it is difficult to get a divorce after a church marriage. The divorce

Opposite: **Arts and crafts from the Altos de Chavón School of Design**

The Legacy of Names

In the United States and Canada, a child born to parents who are married is given one or two first names, usually followed by the surname (last, or family name) of the father. In this way, family history is primarily traced back through the father's side. In the Dominican Republic, however, the system is more complicated.

For example, a man named Carlos Santiago de Fonseca has the first name of Carlos. His father's surname, Santiago, is the name that will be passed on to his children, while his last name is Fonseca, which was his mother's surname. He has a daughter named María, so her childhood name is María Santiago. María meets and marries a man named Eduardo Martín Núñez. Her married name now reads María Santiago de Martín. Two years later she has a son. He is named Pepe, so his full name is Pepe Martín Santiago. Her daughter, Esperanza, is Esperanza Martín Santiago until she marries, when she has the option of taking her husband's name.

Customs of Birth

Many women in the Dominican Republic, especially those who live in rural areas, follow certain guidelines during their pregnancies and childbirth. Most of these traditions are considered superstitious, but they are followed "just in case."

- A pregnant woman must not eat fruit or coconut, or the baby will not breathe properly.
- A pregnant woman should not lift her arms over her head or she will strangle the child with the umbilical cord.
- If anyone walks behind a pregnant woman in her last two months, she will have a difficult labor.

- If a woman clips her child's nails before baptism, the child will grow up to be a thief.
- If you hang a baseball glove on a baby boy's crib, he will become a good baseball player.
- No visitors who have seen the moon are allowed near a woman after childbirth because they will make the new mother sick.

rate is approximately 50 percent, with most separations occurring among couples in their early twenties. It is customary in these cases for the woman to keep the house (if they have one) and the children, with financial support from the father for any legally recognized children.

Families of the upper and middle classes usually choose to have a church wedding. After a long formal engagement, the bride and groom's extended families gather for the service. Afterward they all get to know each other better and greet invited friends at a large, usually elaborate fiesta.

The Family

When two people marry and bring their families together, they increase their collective power. The bond between families in the Dominican Republic is very strong, espe-

An extended family from La Ciénega

cially between blood relatives but also with in-laws. Many people trust only family members and their parish priest. Family members help in times of sickness and financial need. This family solidarity exists in all classes, from the very wealthy, who may owe their money and power to family connections, to the poorest, who may depend on family members just to survive.

The Loss of a Family Member

When a family member becomes seriously ill, relatives, friends, and neighbors gather at the house and help the family care for their loved one. If a person dies, a set of rules must be followed. First, anything in the house that is used to hold water is emptied, so that the living won't drink any water that the dead soul might have bathed in. The whole family gathers near the deceased person and everyone stays until the next day's funeral.

For nine days after the death, called *los nueve días,* only the back door may be used in some rural areas. *Los nueve días* is a time of mourning and tears, wailing and song. Prayers for the soul are frequent, and family members talk continuously of the dead person's virtues. On the one-year anniversary of a death, the family gathers to mourn and remember their loved one's life.

The family unit is also extended to include *compadres*, or godparents. After agreeing to take this responsibility, the *compadre* (godfather) or *comadre* (godmother) is considered essential to the child's upbringing. When a close family friend becomes a godparent, the relationship with the parents changes from casual friendship to a more formal one. *Compadres* must help pay for events such as baptism, marriage, and funerals. Medical care and education are also a responsibility, and the godchild may ask his or her *compadre* or *comadre* for money. *Compadres* are also protective figures who usually spoil the child, who in turn treats godparents with a great deal of love and respect.

The Dominican Way of Celebrating

Dominican people love parties. One of the best-known festivals is Carnival, which originated in medieval Europe as one last bash before the serious forty days of Lent. The major Carnival takes place each year in Santo Domingo, starting along the waterfront and moving its way through the streets. Families travel from across the island to participate in the festivities.

In preparation for the parade, everyone makes elaborate costumes, and huge floats are built and decorated. The most popular costume is that of the *diablo cojuelo*, a devil with power to rid the body of evil. Children make masks portraying this devil and his huge horns and teeth. Each area has its own traditional masks and costumes.

As the procession moves down the street, it passes rows of vendors called *casetas* who play loud merengue music and sell food and souvenirs late into the night. Every major city has its own Carnival customs. The festivities take place every Sunday in February. The best of the best go to Santo Domingo for the final parade, which takes place on Independence Day or the Sunday closest to it.

A parade of devil masks at the Santo Domingo carnival

Night life is a major part of everyone's leisure time. In the cities, Dominicans go to the many clubs and bars, or even to the gambling casinos. There is nearly always music for dancing, and everyone dresses in their best. Outdoors, the sidewalk becomes a dance floor at Christmas and during festivities for the patron saints of some towns. The long stretch of Santo Domingo's waterfront is the setting for an outdoor party during the summer, *Festival del Merengue*, when the best Dominican and Latin American musicians lead the entertainment. In the villages, the single road through town may become the party's base, with anything from radio music to local groups to disk jockeys provided by local businesses. Cars must weave their way carefully between the dancers to get through town.

Friends gathering at a social club in Santiago

Folk Tradition

With such a strong sense of family, Dominicans have always valued oral traditions. In the past, stories and fables were passed down from generation to generation to entertain and instruct the young. Today, television has interfered with this custom, as young and old sit and watch TV instead of talking. Some folk traditions have lived on, however. Many of the folk tales and fables originated in Africa and are the same as those told by slaves in the southern United States. One series of adventures involve Lapén, a cheeky rabbit who gets into scrapes but escapes by using his wits. This character is much like Brer Rabbit, the hero of stories by Joel Chandler Harris, which are based on African-American folk tales.

Dolls and maracas from Puerto Plata

Folk Arts

Handmade crafts, such as the carved calabash, or gourd, are still popular. Dried gourds are often made into ornate masks and containers, or filled with seeds to rattle as *maracas*—musical instruments. Many traditional crafts have survived, even though the product may be manufactured in a less expensive form for tourists.

Pottery figures for Christmas nativity scenes are one of the most famous products of the island, as well as figurines and other decorative pottery items. Most of these are made of an unglazed terra-cotta clay, and their designs may be rough and primitive or crafted in some detail. A creche set may have seven or eight people and an array of animals that include sheep, cows, burros and other local animals. The figures of Joseph and the shepherds often wear sombrero hats.

Women, especially the *campesinas* in rural areas, are also well known for their macramé. These elaborate knotted bags, pocketbooks, and even hammocks are very popular with visitors. Macramé is a cottage craft that can be done easily at home, using string and needing almost no tools, so it costs the artist very little and it brings in some badly needed pesos. Other traditional skills are wood carving, palm weaving, and making jewelry from native coral and seashells. It is common to see young men selling colorful necklaces of shell beads along the beaches.

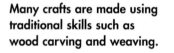

Many crafts are made using traditional skills such as wood carving and weaving.

An Island Beat

On every street corner, in every store, the sound of music puts rhythm into the step of the passersby. This is the land of merengue, where everyone loves its African tom-tom beat and Spanish salsa spirit. Merengue is the most popular form of music and brings crowds together, creating diversion and entertainment for everyone.

Originally, the merengue was performed using the *tambora* (a drum with two ends), the *güira* (scraper), and the accordion. Like all folk music, its sound has changed over the years.

Folkloric dancers and merengue musicians with traditional instruments— a *güira*, an accordion, and a *tambora* (left to right)

In this century the saxophone was introduced, and in the 1960s the salsa beat was mixed into the unique sound. Now, merengue bands also use guitars. The lyrics that go along with the traditional melodies can be about anything from love to politics. The last week of each July, there is a large merengue festival in Santo Domingo where musicians gather from all over the island.

Music in the Dominican Republic is enriched by a wide variety of influences. Nearby Jamaica has contributed the popular sound of reggae. Spanish influences also bring the unmistakable Latin beat and the sounds of guitar. A few folk dances, of native and foreign origin, are still performed on special occasions, using traditional instruments. The island's largest center for music, the National Conservatory for Music and Speech, was built in Santo Domingo in 1949.

Don Pedro Mir, known as "The National Poet"

Literature

For years, only the wealthiest families had the privilege of a formal education. As a result, most literature produced or enjoyed in the Dominican Republic came from the upper classes. Its literary works and style have been heavily influenced by Spain, France, and other European countries. Well-known Dominican writers include Juan Bosch Gaviño, Héctor Inchaustegui Cabral, Salomé Ureña de Henríquez, Pedro Henríquez Ureña, Manuel del Cabral, Don Tomás Morel, and Don Pedro Mir.

Most Dominican literature has reflected the world's artistic trends. The strongest movement within the last century was that of modernism, led by the author Gastón Fernando Deligne. More recent Dominican authors have tried to leave Spanish influences behind and move into a unique Dominican style.

Politics and Literature

Two of the Dominican Republic's presidents have contributed to the island's literature. Juan Bosch Gaviño is considered one of the greatest Dominican writers. Bosch wrote many short stories about his time spent in exile. His political rival, Joaquín Balaguer, is a poet and novelist.

Take Me Out to the Ball Game

In 1891, the neighboring Cubans introduced a sport that would become a way of life. Baseball, brought to Cuba by U.S. troops, is now the number-one Dominican sport. Its widespread play was encouraged by plantation owners who wanted to keep workers occupied during slow seasons. Baseball leagues were formed in the 1920s.

A Player Protests

The most famous "Dominican" baseball player is Satchel Paige, who was born in Mobile, Alabama. In 1937, in protest against the racial segregation of American leagues, he left his American team to play on a team in the Dominican Republic. At that time, black players in the United States could only play in the Negro Leagues. Paige's move focused attention on baseball's policies and inspired the integration of black and white players. It also called the attention of major league scouts to the high quality of Dominican baseball players.

Today, the Dominican Republic is considered the best place for major league players to practice in their off-season. Each year, the leagues send recruiters to the island to find the best players for new contracts. The city of San Pedro de Macorís contributes more professional baseball players than any other town. Every little boy there starts life with a baseball glove hanging on his crib, and is brought up to excel in this sport.

Some Famous Ballplayers from the Dominican Republic

Felipe Alou, manager of the Montreal Expos

Moisés Alou of the Houston Astros

Tony Fernández of the Toronto Blue Jays

Vladimir Guerrero of the Montreal Expos

Wilton Guerrero of the Montreal Expos

Juan Marichal of the San Francisco Giants; inducted into the Baseball Hall of Fame

Pedro Martínez of the Boston Red Sox

Raúl Mondesí of the Los Angeles Dodgers

Manny Ramírez of the Cleveland Indians

Henry Rodríguez of the Chicago Cubs

Juan Samuel of the Toronto Blue Jays

Sammy Sosa (left), outfielder for the Chicago Cubs, with a batting average of .433; named National League Player of the Month in June 1998

Cockfighting

The tradition of cockfighting originated in Spain and, like bullfighting, is now a controversial subject. Gamecocks, called *gallos de pelea*, are bred and trained to have nasty tempers. Owners bring their birds to the site of the fight and, after bets have been made, the birds are put in a ring. The birds have small spurs attached to their legs and fight until one of the birds is defeated (and sometimes killed). The winner is kept for breeding. Although many Dominicans feel that this is a cruel and barbaric tradition that should be stopped, it is still a popular pastime, especially for men in rural areas.

Cockfighting is a controversial sport due to the cruel treatment of the birds, but it is still a popular pastime for men.

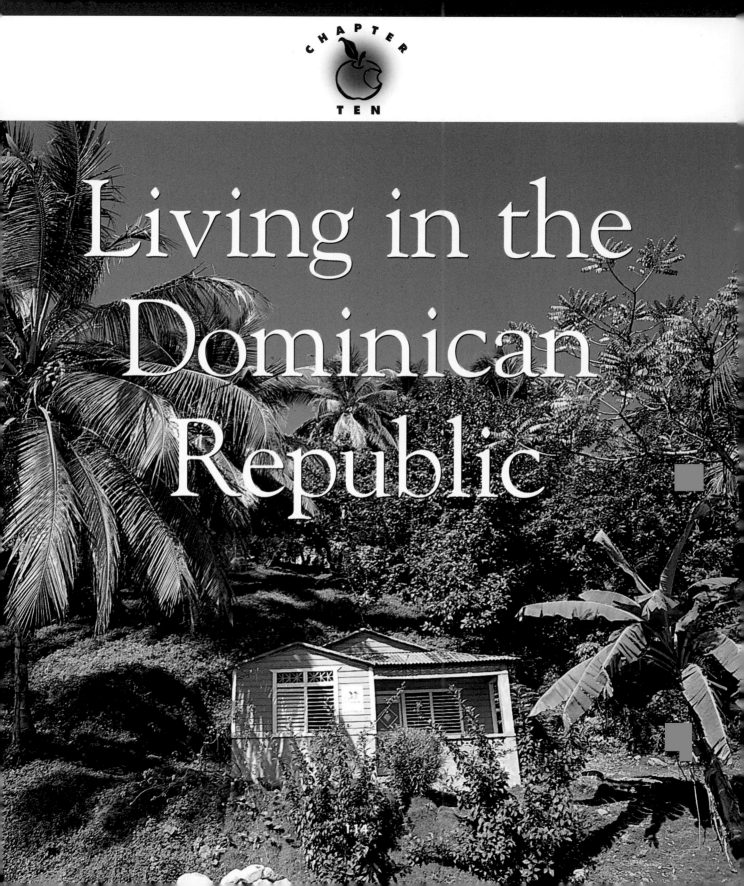

Living in the Dominican Republic

A shopkeeper in Altos de Chavón

Life for Dominicans, although a challenge for many, is faced with optimism and good spirits. Despite a variety of economic and health problems, the people of this beautiful island try to make the best of what they have. Whether they live in the peaceful countryside or the busy city, all Dominicans face life with the help of friends and family.

Dominican Women

Women in the Dominican Republic have a different role than women in the United States or Canada. Today, many women—up to 20 percent—are single mothers who work to support their entire family but they are still regarded in an old-fashioned way. Especially in rural areas, women are expected to be submissive—willing to serve men. Their virtue is important, as well as a mild manner and quiet presence. In return, the men are supposed to protect them.

A young girl of the upper and middle classes must always have a chaperon, usually a male relative such as an uncle or brother, to guard her virtue and her good reputation. This is very important, since virginity until marriage is considered to be extremely important. She is also expected to be quiet, polite, and willing to help in any way she can. As a mother, a woman of any class is respected, and her bond with her child is exceptionally strong throughout life.

In recent years, the public view of women has seen some changes. While President Joaquín Balaguer was in office, he appointed several women to state offices, such as provincial governors. Because employers often prefer female workers, who traditionally work for lower wages, many women are now finding themselves the main support of their household. As a result, women are beginning to have more social and political influence.

Saying Hello

Each culture has its own ways for people to greet one another. These customs depend on age, gender, and how well people know one another. The younger generations in the Dominican Republic greet each other by clasping hands in much the same way as people in the United States and Canada shake hands. Most men also greet each other with a handshake, although if they are close friends, a hug is acceptable. When a man and a woman meet, a swift kiss on the cheek is common. When a woman greets a woman, a kiss on the cheek is the usual greeting. Most of these customs are rooted in Spanish traditions.

Machismo

The most obvious trait among Dominican males is their superiority complex, or *machismo*. This self-image of male strength and control originated in Spain. In order to make themselves feel more secure, men often make bold, overconfident remarks to women. They do this mainly for the benefit of their peers to make themselves seem more important.

In societies where machismo is the traditional male role, women play their own game by flirting. By a glance or the way they walk, they may appear to be interested in a man, just to

A group of Dominican working men posing outside an amber mine

tease him. Dominican women are just as skillful at this game as the men are at *machismo*.

Men are traditionally the head of the family, the major figure of authority. Unlike women, it is widely accepted for a man to have many lovers, both before and after marriage. Affairs are expected, and considered essential to the male image. As long as he takes care of any children of these affairs, his social standing is retained—or even elevated. Sometimes, however, this attitude may lead to divorce.

Young boys have a lot more freedom than young girls. While girls are expected to entertain themselves quietly, dressed up like dolls, the boys run free. In poorer classes, young boys often run around naked. They are not taught to be ashamed of their bodies. These gender roles are learned early in life and become an unquestioned standard.

Home, Sweet Home

Most country people live in a simple home made of whatever materials are available. These houses were once built of palm or pine wood, but palm trees are protected by law today. Many of those older homes are still standing. In dry regions, houses may be built of woven twigs, sometimes reinforced with mud and plaster. Other country homes are made of cement blocks, or blocks and wood. People who can afford them have cement floors; others have dirt floors. Tin or zinc roofs are added when possible, because they last longer. Houses are often painted in bright colors that contrast with those of their neighbors' homes.

Some villages, especially in the mountains, have wooden houses. These homes have one main room with a separate cookhouse so that the building will not get too hot or fill with smoke. Towns usually cluster around some sort of church and one or two tiny stores, which are often the size of a hot dog stand, with a window-counter. A slightly larger town may also have a butcher and a small store or pool hall. Wealthier towns have medical clinics and a few modern conveniences.

The poor who live in the city live in less desirable surroundings. Many houses are nothing more than big cardboard boxes fixed up with any materials that can be found. Much of the low-income housing in Santo Domingo was destroyed in

Many Dominicans enjoy bright-colored houses.

Characteristic country houses of the Samaná Peninsula

beautification efforts, so it is harder to find today, hidden away in corners of the city.

The suburbs are now filling with middle-class houses, which are like small suburban homes in American or Canadian cities. Wealthy city people live in pretty houses with high walls and gates to keep out the lower classes.